Jamaica's Heritage

an untapped res

GW00543850

A PRESERVATION PROPOSAL

by

TOURISM ACTION PLAN LIMITED

in collaboration with

THE JAMAICA NATIONAL HERITAGE TRUST

authors

MARCUS BINNEY   JOHN HARRIS   KIT MARTIN

editor

MARGUERITE CURTIN

THE MILL PRESS
Kingston, Jamaica
1991

Richard Arnell.

Kingston, 2014

A 1991 MILL PRESS PUBLICATION
Second Impression 1993
Third Impression 1995

The MILL PRESS Limited
Constant Spring
Box 167, Kingston 8
JAMAICA, West Indies
Telephone: (809) 925-6886
Facsimile: (809) 931-1301

© *TOURISM ACTION PLAN Limited*
64-70 Knutsford Boulevard
Kingston 5
JAMAICA, West Indies
Telephone: (809) 968-3626 / 968-3441 / 968-1909
Facsimile : (809) 929-5061

TEXT:
Marcus Binney • John Harris • Kit Martin

EDITOR:
Marguerite Curtin

PHOTOGRAPHY:
Marcus Binney • Francis Machin   (United Kingdom)
Jack Tyndale Biscoe • Milton Williams • Kent Reid and others (Jamaica)

NATIONAL LIBRARY OF JAMAICA CATALOGUING IN PUBLICATION DATA

Tourism Action Plan Limited

Jamaica's heritage : an untapped resource. – Rev. ed.

    p. ; ill. ; cm - (Historic heritage series,
ISSN 0799-0170 ; No.1)

ISBN 976 8092 90 4

1.   Historic sites - Jamaica - Conservation and restoration
2.   Historic buildings - Jamaica - Conservation and restoration

I.   Jamaica National Heritage Trust II. Binney, Marcus
III.   Harris, John IV. Martin, Kit   V. Curtin, Marguerite
VI.   Title
       363.69'097292-dc 20

DESIGN AND PRODUCTION
  The Mill Press, Kingston, Jamaica
  Valerie Facey • Executive Editor and Design Consultant

COLOUR SEPARATIONS
  Colour Processors Limited, Kingston, Jamaica

Front cover photo of Fort Balcarres in Falmouth by Milton Williams
Back cover aerial photo of Falmouth by Jack Tyndale Biscoe

Printed in Jamaica by Phoenix Printery

*A view of King Street,
Kingston, Jamaica, looking
north towards the Parade,
c.1844 by Adolphe Duperly.
Note Kingston Parish
Church, with its spire, built
between 1695 and 1701,
destroyed in 1907
earthquake and rebuilt by
1911 as it is today.*

CONTENTS

THE AUTHORS

MARCUS BINNEY, OBE

MARCUS BINNEY is founder and President of SAVE Britain's Heritage. A former editor of *Country Life* magazine, he is presently architecture correspondent of *The Times*, an author and exhibition organiser. He is well-known in Britain for his efforts to salvage buildings and conserve the environment. His determined action has saved noteworthy landmarks while his inspired resourcefulness has transformed many an improbable historic edifice into a viable entity.

JOHN HARRIS, OBE

JOHN HARRIS, for some thirty years, has been an authoritative pioneer figure in the study of architectural history and the connoisseurship of architectural drawings. An historian of art and gardening, he is the author of many books in addition to catalogues for exhibitions which he has organised. He is an adviser to museums and important private collectors and, for over twenty years, as Curator of the Drawings Collection of the Royal Institute of British Architects, he built up the largest and most comprehensive collection of architectural drawings in the world.

KIT MARTIN

KIT MARTIN, trained as an architect and from a family of architectural luminaries, has undertaken the rescue of a series of spectacular problem country houses in England and Scotland, restoring them often from an extreme state of dereliction and converting them as a series of individual family houses. This work has been done on a commercial basis without so much as a penny of Historic Buildings Council grant.

The group at Devon House: From back - l. to r. Kit Martin, Marcus Binney, John Harris, Valerie Facey, Sally Martin, Fay Pickersgill (Executive Director of TAP), Anne Binney and Hon. Maurice Facey (Chairman of TAP). Missing from photo: Eileen Harris and Marguerite Curtin.
PHOTO: Norman D. Hamilton
Courtesy Jamaica Tourist Board

John Harris and Marcus Binney were joint organisers of the exhibition THE DESTRUCTION OF THE COUNTRY HOUSE *at the Victoria & Albert Museum. Kit Martin and Marcus Binney are joint authors of* THE COUNTRY HOUSE: TO BE OR NOT TO BE *and* CHATHAM HISTORIC DOCKYARD – ALIVE OR MOTHBALLED. *All three cooperated on SAVE's first venture overseas,* SAVE GIBRALTAR'S HERITAGE.

MARGUERITE R. CURTIN – EDITOR

MARGUERITE CURTIN is a Jamaican whose life interests are history, art and community development. She studied in the United Kingdom at the University of Wales and Manchester University; she also pursued Publishing in Developing Countries at the Institute of Development Studies in Sussex.

In Jamaica, Miss Curtin has written and edited extensively. In addition, she spent ten years in teaching, a further ten as Education Officer with the Ministry of Education and, from 1987 to 1991, was the Director of Sites, Monuments & Public Education with the Jamaica National Heritage Trust. She is currently Director of Culture at the Ministry of Information and Culture.

HERITAGE TOURISM:

JAMAICA'S PAST – THE GATEWAY TO OUR FUTURE

THERE IS general recognition that Jamaica's heritage is one of the nation's most valuable resources. Not only is this legacy of importance to our people and their pride in themselves, but also it has the additional benefit of being a source of much needed income as a potentially unrivalled tourism product. For this reason, we at Tourism Action Plan Limited (TAP) concentrate a significant portion of our energies on working along with the Government and its agencies, as well as with the private sector on the restoration and improvement of the infrastructure of our towns, villages and historical sites. As well we are encouraging the promotion of our unique artistic creativity which has developed from the melding of the Arawak, European and African cultures. It is critical that this be documented *now* before our invaluable heritage is lost to future generations.

We believe that such efforts will not only enhance the lives of Jamaicans but also help to make our island an outstanding tourism destination. We were delighted, therefore, when Marcus Binney decided to join forces with us on this exciting long term project.

It was in February 1988 that Marcus Binney and friends first came to Jamaica on holiday with their families. All three being persons of extraordinary energy, they were not content to remain idle at the beach so they hired a mini-bus and, with the help of an updated 1888 sugar map, ably navigated themselves across miles of basic roads and remote country parts, exploring the sites and remains of Jamaican great houses, sugar factories and other historic buildings.

The result of this visit was a most pertinent article called *Jamaican Revival* which appeared in the September 1988 issue of *Landscape*, a magazine devoted to historical and environmental preservation.

In March 1990, the Binney, Harris, Martin team came to Jamaica under the auspices of Tourism Action Plan Limited to share their expertise in the preparation of this publication. Their time and effort was a gift to this nation in recognition of our country's historic and artistic heritage which, along with the natural environment, they believe to be Jamaica's most valuable tourism product.

TAP is proud to have merited the assistance of men of such eminence in their field. They have reminded us of the outstanding achievement of our people who, from before the days of slavery, have evolved with dignity as master craftsmen demonstrating an inborn appreciation of good standards and style. Be it the grandest great house or the smallest cabin, it was from the skills of the masons, carpenters and woodworkers that our distinctive artistic architectural expression now called Jamaica-Georgian has developed.

It is in this context that we hope this report will stimulate all Jamaicans to understand the importance and value to Jamaica of the preservation of the island's many remarkable historic areas such as Port Royal, Spanish Town, Falmouth, Rio Bueno, New Seville; the many vintage landmarks of architectural significance and the promotion of its art, theatre, music, dance and ethnic traditions.

Heritage Tourism has the potential to be one of Jamaica's greatest assets. Until now, this source has been virtually untapped: it presents the means to assist in the critical development of the Jamaican economy and to inspire ever increasing benefits for our people.

Hon. Maurice W. Facey, OJ
Chairman
TOURISM ACTION PLAN LIMITED
September 1991

PREFACE

PRESERVATION PAYS

Historic buildings, quite apart from their intrinsic value and beauty, are a major economic resource and an irreplaceable capital asset, contributing significantly through tourism to earnings of foreign exchange, to local employment and prosperity, and to central government taxation.

All too often the case for conserving historic buildings goes by default because of the costs involved and a lack of appreciation – and readily available evidence – of the economic benefits to be derived from conservation through tourism. Admission fees can rarely cover the cost of maintenance, repairs and opening, but, if the wider benefits are taken into account, such as the custom attracted to hotels, restaurants, cafés, pubs, shops and parking, then the viability of conservation projects takes on a new perspective.

In Britain [for example] the Exchequer receives very considerable sums in taxation resulting from spending by people visiting and enjoying Britain's architectural heritage. In 1989 alone, £3 billion was realised through tourism, and indications are that Britain's architectural heritage was one of the main reasons for visiting the country.

Money spent on conservation is a sensible national investment producing a measurable return in terms of employment, increased trade, foreign exchange and taxation. Conservation is not a fad or a fetter or a curse: it is an essential part of developing a good tourism product and should be seen as a stimulating challenge.

As a result of the tourism generated by historic buildings, small country villages can continue as viable economic units without the need for manufacturing industries which would spoil their character. Considerable employment is created in the hotel trade which is associated with the higher spending propensity of the more educated tourists who visit historic buildings. Country crafts are given a better chance of survival, and local residents can enjoy a more extensive range of facilities than would otherwise be possible.

Historic buildings and areas are tangible economic assets, producing a measurable financial return. The logical conclusion must be that they should be the subject of a planned investment of years as are all other productive assets – not only to ensure their continued viability but to develop new potential.

From the book
PRESERVATION PAYS
by Marcus Binney

A view of the Kingston Barracks c. 1844 by Adolphe Duperly. One of several similar architectural type barracks built in the 1700s and early 1800s in Jamaica

NB All black and white photos of Duperly prints are by Kent Reid courtesy the Facey/Boswell Trust Collection.

DISCOVER JAMAICA

1

THE ARCHITECTURAL HERITAGE – *THE PROPOSAL*

THIS REPORT is intended to enhance plans already in process in Jamaica while complementing studies previously written. Extensive research and reports have already dealt with the three most obvious and important historic areas, Port Royal, Spanish Town and New Seville. Our purpose is to call attention to the many other aspects of Jamaica's inherent historic potential for which results can be achieved quickly, at minimal cost and which can eventually link the entire island as one remarkable historic landmark.

The proposal, therefore, is the result of a brief but intensive tour of Jamaica's exceptional architectural heritage. Our visit was all the more enjoyable because of the Jamaican hospitality which we received. We discovered so much about the island which the vast majority of tourists never have the opportunity to encounter. A large number of these visitors probably never leave their hotel complex except, perhaps, on a group tour to some attractions.

At present, holiday provision in Jamaica centres on sun, sea and sand. These are marvellous, but are offered by every other Caribbean island, as well as numerous other destinations. In order to foster the prosperity of Jamaica, and to promote return visits, holiday-makers should be encouraged to explore the island, seeing the rich architecture, scenery, trees, flora and fauna, much of which is not to be found elsewhere in the world.

In a short time, we were also able to visit a number of plantation houses, as well as observe numerous cottages and vernacular buildings of a distinctive character. While we are very conscious that we saw only a fraction of what is to be found, we were impressed by the number of fascinating and absorbing places that it was often possible to see within just a few miles of each other.

A view of the Ordinance Yard from Port Royal Street, c. 1844, by Adolphe Duperly. Note ship's masts and evidence of tree planting for shade and beautification in the city of Kingston as far back as the early 19th century.

THE HERITAGE TRAIL

OUR PRINCIPAL PROPOSAL is that a *Jamaica Heritage Trail* should be established, linking in practical segments all significant towns and villages islandwide, encouraging visitors to explore the island. The need is not only to provide literature and promotion, but also to initiate a number of projects bonded by a common theme, so that once people start on the trail, they will want to seek more and more.

As an accompaniment to the stalwart areas of thematic historical importance, Port Royal, Spanish Town, and New Seville, the common theme of the *Heritage Trail* is the role of the island in the eighteenth century as the world's largest and most important sugar producer.

A surprising number of spectacularly sited great houses and sugar factories survive from that era, many with some original equipment and machinery. Along with these aspects go the small ports and quays where hogsheads of sugar were stored in warehouses and then loaded on to ships to sail across the Atlantic.

The forgotten town of Falmouth is a case in point. An architectural gem, it is potentially one of the finest and, if rescued immediately, paradoxically one of the easiest areas with which to achieve quick results. Historically, apart from its own inborn colourful past, there is international fascination through the association with the famous literary Barrett and Browning families, and the little known fact that Robert Browning's great-great-grandfather was a shoemaker and tavern keeper of Port Royal. One cannot help comparing Falmouth's possibilities with the proven success of Colonial Williamsburg in the USA. Being in close proximity to Montego Bay, the principal entry point for visitors to the island, Falmouth is, more often than not, the first location passed through after leaving the airport. Imagine the visitor's first impressions of Jamaica after experiencing a restored town of Falmouth.

A remarkable amount of rich and varied architecture from this period survives. Much of it, however, is in a very fragile state, and in danger of complete obliteration unless the problem is immediately tackled by Government together with input from private enterprise.

In addition to the historic towns, the *Heritage Trail* should show visitors some of the great houses and use a selected few as restaurants and small hotels furnished, as far as possible, as they might originally have been. The *Trail* should include visits to one or two sugar factories which are in partial working order, and exhibitions to show how sugar was manufactured. Similar exhibitions are needed to show how the small ports and wharfs operated in the eighteenth century.

Our proposal is that the visitor should see a series of sites showing the whole process from canefield to factory buildings and finally to a section of shore-line in Falmouth with a restored jetty.

Once people are on the *Heritage Trail* they will also be drawn inland to see the countryside and enjoy the spectacular landscape and be able to visit a number of local communities where Jamaican crafts can be seen and purchased in restored rustic vernacular buildings.

In the case of each main landmark or village on the *Trail*, the principal building should include a small museum or exhibition where people could absorb a short history of the property or area; old photographs showing the life and growth of the estate or community could be displayed. Most important, there should also be a display about other sites on the *Heritage Trail* with complementary literature and maps available.

A series of plantation houses – perhaps three in Phase One – should be restored and presented to form major focal points on the *Heritage Trail*. For ease of operation we have chosen three estates already in Government ownership, three great houses in the parish of St. Ann, which, we believe, could in the near future make a dramatic contribution to the proposed *Heritage Trail*. These are:

1) *Roaring River*
2) *Minard*
3) *Seville.*

All three are close to the main North Coast tourist route but each takes people a few steps into the countryside to enjoy the landscape. They are all different in character and thereby complement each other. Roaring River house has an Edwardian swagger in its lofty proportions; Minard is a significant great house of Jamaica-Georgian style on a beautiful up-country cattle property; Seville is an historically important great house with spectacular views looking out at the coastline where Christopher Columbus first arrived in Jamaica in 1494 and where, on his fourth and last voyage in 1503, he was compelled to beach his two vessels and remain as an unwilling visitor along with his men for one year and five days until finally rescued.

Port Maria, the capital of the Parish of St. Mary as it was in 1820 according to James Hakewill, artist and architect visiting at that time. Morgan's 1670s 'lookout' at Firefly, where Noel Coward is buried, is at the top of the mountain on the extreme left. Note Cabaritta Island which may have been part of the early settlement of Melilla.
Courtesy Facey/Boswell Trust collection

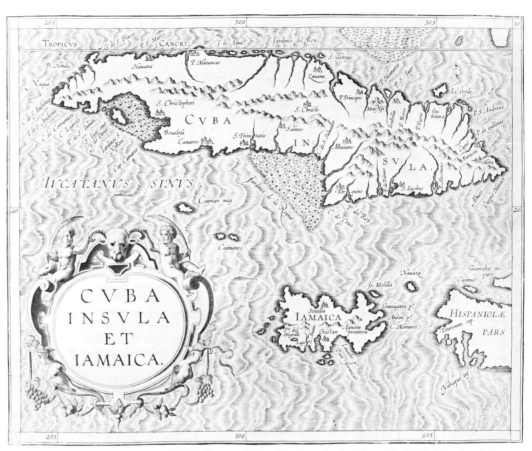

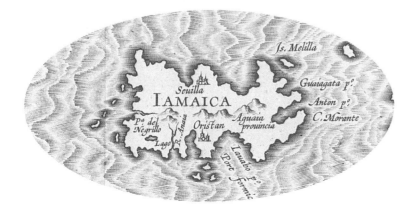

1597 Wytfliet map of Cuba, Jamaica and part of Hispaniola. Detail of Jamaica shows settlements of Seville and Oristan (now Bluefields) with Spanish settlements indicated. Seville, founded in 1509, fifteen years after the arrival of Christopher Columbus, was in 1534 abandoned and the capital moved to Villa de la Vega later called Spanish Town by the British. The inaccurate shape of the island and the omission of Villa de la Vega shows how out of date this map was in 1597 by which time many Spanish communities had been established. Scholars debate whether Melilla, here shown as a separate island, was located at Port Maria or at Annotto Bay. It is contended that Melilla was probably an extensive Arawak habitation governed by the great cacique Huareo.
PHOTO: Kent Reid courtesy M. & V. Facey Collection.

THE FALMOUTH RESTORATION PROGRAMME

2

INTRODUCTION

FALMOUTH is a model Georgian town that deserves international recognition. In terms of Jamaican heritage only the superb Spanish Town Square equals it in architectural merit. Falmouth's unique possession is the ancillary infill of a Georgian town that has been destroyed elsewhere. Laid out in the late 1770s as a model town, Falmouth is remarkably intact and unparalleled in the entire Caribbean.

The fascination of Falmouth is that it is all in one piece. Built between 1790 and 1830 it fell into a steady decline after this short period of roughly forty years. The new larger steamships could not easily use the harbour: later, the railway extensions of 1894 which went to Montego Bay excluded Falmouth, thus the pattern of decline continued into the twentieth century and to this day.

Though many of the Georgian buildings are now dilapidated, there has been relatively little development. In Falmouth one gets the real sense of scale of an eighteenth century town, for it is not only the large buildings which have survived but also many one-room and two-room cabins, and even smaller buildings such as outdoor kitchens.

Records of the early sale of plots are of significance: in 1775 Edward Barrett, the owner of Cinnamon Hill as well as the land on which Falmouth was to develop, sold lot 34 to two carpenters, Samuel Reeves and John Sylvester, both mulattos. Obviously the men were proposing to build a house for sale or lease to a sugar planter. Although laid out on the standard Renaissance grid pattern (a grid of 6 x 6 streets), Falmouth's frontages do not boast an architectural display beyond, perhaps, an open arcade of plain Tuscan columns, some quoins, and key-stone windows. All this work was capable of being executed by carpenters, such as Reeves and Sylvester, possessed of no more than a simple pattern or design book of instructions, such as one of the many produced in England by William and John Pain.

An excellent study of Falmouth, published twenty years ago by the Georgian Society of Jamaica and now reprinted, is illustrated by an Adolphe Duperly daguerreotype showing an old view of the town as seen from the church tower, c. 1844. This shows many of the gardens, or yards as they are called in Jamaica, planted luxuriantly with trees and shrubs. Tall palm trees provide important accents, but the range of different types of trees is conspicuous.

The old print also shows that much of Falmouth's trim and tidy appearance was due to neat fencing around the edge of each plot.

A view of Market Street in Falmouth, Jamaica c.1844.by Adolphe Duperly: a gem of a Georgian town in urgent need of restoration, Falmouth is considered equal to Colonial Williamsburg in Virginia, USA.

NB All colour photos of Falmouth by Milton Williams. These include two 1991 Festival Award Winners.

A very faded photograph of Falmouth c. 1890. Note abundant trees and foliage.
PHOTO: Jamaica Archives courtesy Allan Keeling

A view of Falmouth (from the Church Tower) by Adolphe Duperly c. 1844. Note neat houses, fencing, planted trees and shrubs.
PHOTO: Martin Mordecai courtesy of University of the West Indies Library

From the print it is evident that there were several varieties of fence and boundary walls. In Falmouth today quite a number of boundary walls of colonial date can still be found as well as occasional stretches of earlier fencing.

Although subject to decay and grievous damage by hurricanes, principally those of 1944 and 1988, Falmouth has survived, ironically, due to neglect. The seaside-based tourist flow has by-passed it and left it stranded like a ship, high and dry on some promontory beach. Little has been done to bring Falmouth into tourism focus and this is a blessing in disguise. But she cannot survive much longer as the processes of gradual decay will soon become irreversible.

For the smaller, even more than larger buildings in Falmouth, this decay is especially worrying. No town of the Georgian era besides Falmouth has retained its ancillary and dependent buildings, most of which were slave quarters attached to the planters' town houses. At Colonial Williamsburg these had to be reconstructed from archaelogical evidence, but here in Falmouth many are intact and are a remarkable display of what might be called the *cabin style* of Georgian vernacular architecture. Herein lies the supreme architectural importance of the model town of Falmouth.

Elsewhere in the world, these would receive recognition and there would be international pleas for their preservation. Had it been in the USA, lavish monies would have been spent upon the town's restoration (for example, as at Deerfield or Colonial Williamsburg) and in Europe it would have become a *ville d'art*, venerated for its perfection as a small Georgian town.

Falmouth compares well with Colonial Williamsburg, Virginia, where much of the charm lies in the reconstructed every-day life of the town. At Falmouth, on the other hand, originals survive. Williamsburg, with some one million visitors a year, rates as one of the world's top heritage attractions: just ten percent of that number of visitors would transform Falmouth's prospects. Impressive results could be achieved with proper management and imaginative marketing.

HISTORIC AREA

FOR HISTORICAL purposes and the necessary field examination the plan of the town can be divided into two principal areas

1) *The central grid bounded to the west by Pitt street and to the east by Market Street; south by George Street and north by Rodney Street.*

In all cases there is an overflow of one block that fades out into unplanned streets, and a block's width between Rodney and Charlotte Streets to the north adjoining Fort Balcarres. In this grid can be located the William Knibb Church (rebuilt 1948); the 'Georgian' style box Presbyterian Church of 1840 reconstructed after the hurricane of 1903; the early nineteenth century Baptist Manse of simple Gothic fenestration and most of the planters' houses.

2) *The area of Fort Balcarres with the Barracks of 1811, now given over to the Falmouth All Age School.*

Here is the gun bastion and the magazine, and the handsome 1838 house on the corner of Charlotte and King Street. This area is a crucial but unused area.

CONSERVATION AREA

INITIALLY, we thought the designated area should be quite small and act as a pilot project. However, we have decided that if this was successful other streets would be left waiting too long for their turn. This could produce an early blight on the project in which no improvements, or the wrong improvement, would be carried out. Given the importance and fragility of the whole town, it is crucial, therefore, to encourage sensitive work across the whole area.

As well as overall improvements to smaller buildings, we feel that a few prominent buildings should be restored to a high standard. These would act as a catalyst and demonstrate a true sense of purpose in the project and that change was really underway.

The key buildings chosen, of which there are five, should all have some public use or be accessible to the public. The individual projects could be financed by different private or public bodies. For example, a leading company could sponsor one building with which it may have had historical associations.

Above: Colonades at the corner of Market Street and Duke Street. This fine building is gradually being stripped of its detail. Note the eaves where restoration of the traditional cornice should be encouraged. At one time the upper floor of this building was used for the Court.

Right: Plan of Falmouth from 1954 Aerosurvey. Note Fort Balcarres and the Barracks at northern tip of the town.

MARKET STREET

CLEARLY, MARKET STREET is the street which the visitors should turn down initially to explore the town. Three of five key buildings are in Market Street. With these first three buildings improved to a good standard, people in adjoining streets will be all the more eager to take up grants and to start work on their own buildings.

THE BARRETT HOUSE AND ENVIRONS

I N THE SAME WAY that Minard great house in the parish of St. Ann should be a show plantation house, the residence of Edward Barrett in Falmouth should be a show town house. The building is not particularly large but has very interesting architectural detail. The aim would be to show a fine town house and the way it functioned as well as to present a museum about the role that the house and the Barrett family played in the story of a town created when the prosperity of the sugar planter was at its zenith.

Falmouth's story will then be conveyed to the townspeople, including school children, and visitors alike. Thus a fuller and more graphic picture of the island's economic and social history will be presented and Falmouth's place in this context better appreciated.

It is understood that a buyer sympathetic to conservation has acquired the large, derelict site to the east of the Barrett House. Here there is the potential for developing a very attractive garden with wonderful views along the seashore. The warehouse facing the sea is an ideal space for a large restaurant serving traditional food. It would cater for parties of people, including those on bus tours. Here there would be comfortable areas to sit and have a drink, as well as pleasant gardens and good food. All this would operate in close co-operation with the museum on the opposite side of the street.

The rest of this site is of crucial importance. Behind the single storey wall opposite the Barrett House there should be a two-storey residential development. The crazy-paving pointing which disfigures the wall should be removed; the stone wall could form the base or ground floor with a first floor of wooden construction and a verandah with shingle roof.

The site opposite the Barrett House should be sympathetically redeveloped for housing. The existing single story stone wall should be retained and surmounted by a timber first floor with a verandah and traditional fenestration and roof pitch. Quite a number of small houses could be created in an L-plan layout with views across a courtyard to the sea.

The Barrett House, Market Street. One of the five key buildings which must be restored in the first phase of the Falmouth Restoration Project. It should become a show-house with an exhibition illustrating the history of this fine Georgian town.

The warehouse adjoining the Barrett House overlooks what could be a delightful garden by the sea. This is the perfect site for the principal buffet restaurant in Falmouth, serving as a base for day visitors. It should cater to both individuals and larger groups and have a shop selling maps and plans.

Houses in this position would have the benefit of sea views. Further houses on these lines could be constructed in the ruined shells of warehouses standing at right angles to Market Street, facing directly out to sea. A scheme on these lines would also be an excellent opportunity to show how new buildings can be designed to complement the existing streetscape.

THE BAPTIST MANSE (1798)

THIS CUT-STONE building was built as a masonic hall but was later sold to meet debts incurred in its construction. It is the second key building in a very prominent position on the west side of Market Street. It is visible from Water Square in front of the Market House.

Owned by the Baptists, it is understood that its governing body would like to see some public benefit, preferably associated with the work of the church, emerging from any scheme of restoration and re-use.

It is suggested that the building should be repaired and opened to the public with an exhibition on the struggle for Emancipation.

The story of Emancipation is closely tied to the fortunes of the sugar trade. The Non-conformist churches played a vital role in both Britain and Jamaica in bringing about an end to the slave trade (1807) and finally slavery itself in 1834.

An exhibition on these lines would, therefore, be of interest to visitors and an important teaching tool for schools. It is proposed that the large upstairs room should be equipped as a meeting room for use by schools and other groups. This project is suitable for sponsorship partly from the commercial sector and partly from church or charitable sources – including Free Church sources in Britain and North America.

The Baptist Manse in Market Street should be restored in the first phase as a demonstration project. This could provide a mixture of community space and facilities for visitors and school children. It could be part of the Emancipation Trail.

Above: The Cox House in Market Street. This is the third key building that should be restored. Badly damaged by Hurricane Gilbert it lends itself to use as a small restaurant in an attractively restored historic interior. Its central location is ideal for such a use.

Right: At the back of the house is a potentially delightful garden where guests could sit in the shade and sip rum punches.

17

THE COX HOUSE

THIS FINE HOUSE which was badly damaged in the 1988 hurricane is urgently in need of repair. It stands half-way along Market Street backing on to the court house. It is in an excellent position to serve as a restaurant, where people could eat in its pleasant back garden. This restaurant would be different from the larger restaurant proposed for the warehouse site near the sea.

More intimate and expensive, it would give visitors the opportunity to eat at leisure in restored period rooms.

The Cox House site, which was originally one block long, is crucial to the structure of Market Street, the key street in the Falmouth town layout. The hurricane damage will prove to be irreversible unless priority is given to this house immediately.

The Tharp House, now a Tax and Customs office. It is in a fine position overlooking the sea and has excellent architectural detail. It could be sold by the Government for careful restoration and conversion as a small hotel. It is most important that the waterside is tidied up and landscaped as an attractive place from which to view the sea and the jetties.

THE THARP HOUSE

THIS ELEGANT house on the sea-front overlooking the remains of jetties where hogsheads of sugar and puncheons of rum were loaded, was one of three houses in Falmouth owned by John Tharp (1744-1804) the proprietor of Good Hope, Trelawny. Tharp was one of the largest slave-owners in Jamaica. It is proposed that the house be restored and converted into a small privately run hotel with restaurant. The house retains quite a number of original features such as cornices. With the removal of temporary partitions and with sympathetic redecoration it could become an attractive historic interior which would be much enjoyed by visitors.

Currently, the yard behind the house is used by the Public Works Department as a supply depot. It could however be attractively landscaped and the jetty reconstructed. This could also serve as an anchorage for visiting yachts and as a starting point for short boat trips around the harbour. Once again, this is a project which could be carried out by a private individual or commercial investor.

NO. 1 THARP STREET

IT WOULD BE very advantageous to have the exhibition centre of Falmouth's architectural heritage at No. 1 Tharp Street, opposite the old foundry, the town's principal landmark. Well restored and freshly painted, these offices would be a strategic spot for the centre.. A community architect could then show residents photographs of the best way to carry out repairs and take them to the adjoining workshops.

The Falmouth Restoration Project, now located at 16 Market Street, might also be incorporated with the exhibition centre.

An interesting example of a single storey cottage in King Street giving Falmouth its unique scale. It could form a model for the design and detailing of inexpensive new small houses.

Trelawny Street. A good tradtional house in urgent need of repair. Note the horizontal boarding, another possible treatment for street boundaries.

Jalousie window in Newton Street. Money is being spent on a new extension. Advice and a modest grant, however, would have achieved the right details.

19 Queen Street. One or two people are beginning to take pride in their tradtional houses. Imagine the pleasure of walking round and finding more houses proudly maintained like this.

An attractive cottage on the corner of Lower Harbour and King Streets with a tradtional detached kitchen. Notice the importance of tidying up street boundaries.

41 Duke Street. Colourful and decorative detail in urgent need of repair.

This new cabin in King Street would cost no more to build if copied from traditional buildings. As it is, though the scale is right, it detracts from the character of the area because roof pitch and fascia, door and window detail are incorrect. It would be very easy for the traditional type of house to be prefabricated in the joinery shops which are proposed as part of the Falmouth Restoration Project.

33 Duke Street. In this house on the main street through Falmouth, the owner has enjoyed retaining and showing off all the traditional detail. He has needed more space, which has been discreetly arranged to the rear, and which does not affect the street facade.

Cottage in Rodney Street. Another good example of a small house where restoration of traditional detail is urgently required. Being unaltered it is an example of the type of building that might be allowed on infil sites. The boundary wall is an eyesore and needs attention.

House at the corner of Charlotte Street and King Street near Fort Balcarres. This is an important building on a key site. The owner intends to carefully restore the building as a small hotel, following hurricane damage. There are a number of other buildings which could be similarly restored as guest houses and bed and breakfast amenities. Repairs have progressed slowly but imagine the difference if the local authority had tidied up the open space between the house and the sea and the owner had been offered a grant towards the repair of external detail and roof, and had the help of the community architect and did not feel a lone pioneer but knew his restoration formed part of an overall strategy to regenerate the town. As a result of the Falmouth Restoration Programme, loans might be more easily available and owners would have the further incentive of competing in the annual Falmouth award scheme proposed here.

The house being restored by a concerned citizen is a good example of the way traditional character can be retained. Great visual improvements could be made by giving a high level of grant for repairs and rebuilding of traditional street boundaries, such as fences and walls. People should be encouraged to 'infil' vacant plots with carefully designed traditional materials and details for windows, doors and gables. Inappropriate infil must not be allowed.

An important pair of houses in King Street with good surviving detail. When owners want to carry out improvements they must be encouraged by good advice from the community architect, the example of the permanent exhibition, and a financial contribution to repair and retain existing features and character in keeping with the overall image of the whole town.

SHOPPING

THE RESTORATION of the old Albert George Market (built in 1894) has already demonstrated that historic restoration projects can be a commercial success. This project is in a strategically placed building which everyone who passes through Falmouth is likely to see. The newly repaired and repainted clock is a major eye-catcher.

The covered market gives shade to a considerable number of small shops and a meeting area under its roof.

These shops are housed in small cabins of 700 square feet and are of much more potential interest to visitors than large stores. Their dimensions, interestingly, are very similar to the small traditional kiosk shops scattered around Falmouth streets. The success of the market restoration shows that Falmouth's traditional kiosk shops, suitably spruced up, could have a role in serving visitors and provide an opportunity for local people to benefit directly from tourism.

An example of the traditional mini-market in Queen Street.

Shopping in Falmouth c. 1890. Names on buildings include Variety Hall, Delgado Bros, Italian Warehouse, Our Store and The Gladstone.
PHOTO: *Jamaica Archives courtesy Allan Keeling*

Above and below:
Tavern at 33 Queen Street. The small taverns, like the kiosks, are a vital part of the character of the place where local people and tourists can share a cool drink together. We visited this small pub which is the kind of place that visitors might like to visit and where they would always receive a warm Jamaican welcome.

The small shops in wooden kiosks are a distinctive feature and must be encouraged. They would benefit dramatically from inclusion on a town heritage trail, and could sell drinks and ice creams to the visitors. As incomes increase operators must have the incentive of small grants to repair and repaint their shops in traditional fashion.

Fort Balcarres, Falmouth:
The cannon should be a focal point of
an attractively planted seaside walk.

Restoration at the back of
the school is not so important
immediately, but should be
part of the long term plan.

The school is another
public building with an
important street front. It
was originally built in 1811
as the barracks at Fort
Balcarres. A facelift and
the removal of the
disfiguring concrete
walkway is essential. It
could be replaced by timber
construction, more in
keeping with the profile of
the original building.

Abbey Villa is in a key location opposite the church and desperately needs minor facelift treatment.

The burnt out bakery at the corner of Pitt Street and Duke Street. Many people already stop at the elegant 18th century church undergoing restoration. The old bakehouse would be an excellent location for a café selling ice-cream, with washrooms for tourists and an orientation room with photographs, maps and plans. Here people could be introduced to the many things to see and encouraged to explore the restaurants in the historic area and visit the museums and show houses.

The Anglican Church at Falmouth built c. 1795 – an example of classic Georgian architecture.

STRATEGIES

THE PLANNED FALMOUTH Restoration Project should be based on a series of strategies such as those set out herein which could be developed concurrently over a ten year period.

A traditional street boundary. Beyond is the doctor's house in Duke Street which is being carefully restored.

GRANTS – Strategy 1

In the rural areas of Scotland where conservation schemes (known as *town schemes*) involve small and very modest houses – often belonging to people with very limited means – such an approach has been very successful.

Even if the owner does nothing more than maintain his property he is indeed contributing to the survival of the traditional street scene. As soon as he starts to spend his own money, a grant is made available (normally 25% to 30% of the cost) for work on the exterior of the building for decorative features and finishes as well as for roof repairs, painting and woodwork. Experience shows that almost all owners take up the offer, agreeing to conform to specific standards of workmanship and details required. It is all too easy having lived in a place for a lifetime to take its beauty for granted. Conservation schemes in Britain, however, demonstrate that once townspeople see that something is actually happening, intense civic pride develops.

In Falmouth a considerable number of houses, large and small, are owner-occupied. Although many of these dwellings are still untouched, in recent times alterations and 'improvements' are beginning to happen quite rapidly. People are starting to spend, in some cases, quite significant sums on their property. It is crucial, therefore, that expenditure be directed in the right way and that owners be made to understand that an increase in tourism

Water Square in Falmouth c. 1890 with the fountain, looking south toward the hills. The market is off to the left or east of the fountain.
PHOTO: Jamaica Archives courtesy Allan Keeling

will help to revive the town and in turn benefit *them*. Over a period of time the value of their own property will also increase.

Strategy 2 - CONTROLS

Once the grant scheme is underway and the public understands the benefit of the system, it will want controls strictly upheld in the interests of the town. It is important, therefore, that where alterations are carried out without consent and with incorrect detail, that the work be redone correctly. Examples must be made. Usually enforcement action is only necessary in one or two cases to ensure that further work is carried out to proper standards. Sometimes just the threat of action may suffice as a stimulus.

The Jamaica National Heritage Trust is the controlling government body to which such works must be referred for approval. With an injection of funding and a plan for properly supervised restoration, it would be possible for the Trust to enforce its legal control of listed properties and those that should be protected.

The corner of Newton Street and Cornwall Street. On the left, money has been spent on alterations to the ground floor of a traditional house, thus damaging its character. At small cost this could almost certainly have been prevented by grants and free architectural advice. The adjoining house has unusual detail worth preserving.

EXHIBITION AND ADVICE CENTRE –
Strategy 3

A permanent exhibition needs to be established, illustrating the architectural features of the town, and pointing out its special characteristics, as well as showing good examples of restoration. It should include a first-class photographic display, including examples of traditional details so that people are encouraged to repair and/or copy them.

THE COMMUNITY ARCHITECT – *Strategy 4*

For as little as half a day a week a restoration architect would man the exhibition, explaining to the townspeople procedures for application forms. Standards and details of workmanship required for grants, would also be discussed with the architect.

The conservation architect must, therefore, be someone who understands the techniques of traditional construction, mortars and pointing, thus ensuring that the work is done authentically and to a good standard. The architect should also be able to relate sympathetically to the local populace.

At our first meeting in Falmouth which was called by the Chamber of Commerce, we received an encouraging signal that a conservation scheme on these lines would work: a local shop-keeper who wished to restore her house correctly, as she remembered it had been originally with the right windows, asked how she should go about obtaining advice to do this.

While walking around the historic area, we came across many examples of people spending money on older buildings. The need now is to ensure that any improvements or repairs are in keeping with the character of the town.

New House in Queen Street. New houses must not be allowed in the historic district unless they are of traditional design. There is a large number of infil sites and unless new buildings are of sympathetic design the scale and character of the town will be steadily destroyed.

House at 15 King Street. Numerous photographs of traditional details such as this should be displayed in a permanent exhibition adjoining the community architect's office so that people are encouraged to repair and copy them in future.

RESTORATION WORKSHOPS – *Strategy 5*

As restoration gathers pace it is likely that a number of small businesses will be established to undertake work – joiners, carpenters, painters, roofers. It is desirable to encourage this process as much as possible and this could be done by making workshop space available in buildings that are currently empty. One building which would be eminently suitable for such a purpose is the roofless shell behind the old foundry in Old Harbour Street – another distinctive town market. This has the potential advantage of being immediately behind the building on the corner of Tharp Street which is being proposed for the exhibition of Falmouth's architectural heritage. If this scheme proved successful, more space would be available in other disused buildings to the east along Market Street and other important areas.

The corner of Rodney Street and King Street. A good example of traditional fencing which could be one of a number of types used in the restoration.

These workshops should be let at a nominal rent to small businesses and self-employed craftsmen producing such items as correctly detailed sash windows, doors, staircases etc.

It is envisaged that local joinery firms and tradesmen will take the opportunity to learn about restoration standards and techniques and be able to make correctly detailed items. Besides being a profitable source of trade and employment for local people, these workshops would be valuable for restoration projects elsewhere in the island.

NEW BUILDINGS – Strategy 6

There remains in much of the historic area of Falmouth quite a number of derelict sites. Some have begun to be developed unsympathetically; this will mar efforts being made by the people who are carefully restoring neighbouring houses.

Any new buildings should, therefore, meet certain essential requirements:

a) *They must be well sited in relation to the size and shape of the plot. Here they should often take a cue from neighbouring buildings with smaller houses; the fronts are likely to be close to the street, although on larger plots they may be set further back.*

b) *It is vital that new buildings adopt the traditional roof pitch.*

c) *Timber will obviously harmonize well where nearby buildings are timber clad but paintwork can also be used as a means of blending new houses with the street scene, though this does not mean that only subdued colours are admissible.*

Though there are quite a number of new buildings that are out of keeping with the historic area, it is encouraging that there has been relatively little amalgamation of plots. It is vital that as far as possible the original site plots are retained. This, as much as height restrictions, will ensure that the town retains its Georgian scale.

A series of planning policies should, therefore, be introduced to control the character of new development.

a) *Site amalgamation should be resisted.*

b) *The height of new buildings should be restricted to two storeys.*

c) *All new buildings should have roofs of traditional pitch.*

Having established these policies, the number of vacant sites allows considerable space for expansion in the future.

Many of the streets of Falmouth suffer from a plethora of makeshift fencing – much of it rusting corrugated iron – which owners have put up around their properties.

One of the delights of Virginia's Colonial Williamsburg is the variety of attractive wooden fences surrounding the properties. Virtually all of these are reconstructions carried out after careful excavation revealing the size, shape and spacing of different post holes. Williamsburg's experience could be valuable to Falmouth and the good news is that simple wooden fences which will give so much character to the town can be put up cheaply and simply. It is important to avoid too much uniformity. The old print shows a considerable variation of paling. Elements such as fencing must also be protected and recorded.

19 King Street. Mr. Arthur Dyke's house is another example of a careful restoration already in progress. Quite major work has been carried out, but sashes, jalousies, and doors have either been repaired or carefully replaced. The only place where new windows have crept in is at the rear, but these are to scale and proportion to the cottage. The restored street front is a splendid example of what an individual owner can achieve.

A FALMOUTH AWARD SCHEME — *Strategy 8*

In Europe the conservation of historic buildings is so well established that a large number of award schemes have been established. Jamaica already has an excellent national scheme on these lines sponsored by a local paint company. It is felt that Falmouth would, however, profit from the introduction of its own annual Award Scheme for the best restoration scheme in the town. As well as a small plaque which could be displayed on the winning building, there should be a cash prize.

A focal point in the town, the court house is an impressive classical building which needs to be regularly repaired and painted. Reconstructed after a fire in 1926, it was originally built in 1815.

THE ROLE OF THE PUBLIC SECTOR — *Strategy 9*

It is essential that the public sector plays its part in the Falmouth Restoration Project. This can be done in three ways by landscaping public open spaces, by planting trees and by smartening up public buildings.

(a) Landscaping

In the heart of Falmouth the little public square in front of the court house provides a classic example both of what has been done, and what needs to be done: to the east is an attractive and well-maintained small garden – the war memorial with neatly cut grass and flowering shrubs; to the west of the court house, however, the border is still filled with broken tiles and debris from the 1988 hurricane. There needs to be, therefore, a comprehensive clean-up of public areas such as this. Thereafter, they must be kept clean and free from rubbish and, where appropriate, planted with grass and shrubs.

(b) Tree Planting

Tree planting programmes should be introduced both along the streets and on adjacent open sites. The introduction of greenery will dramatically transform the entire town.

(c) Public Buildings

The court house, the police station, and the post office are examples of important buildings in key positions, which for a small outlay could be given a dramatic facelift. What is needed is straightforward repair of peeling plaster-work and repainting which should highlight the architectural forms of the buildings.

Strategy 10 – JAMAICA PUBLIC SERVICE CO. LTD. AND JAMAICA TELEPHONE CO. LTD.

As buildings are restored and public spaces are replanted, the mess of electric wires and poles that now exists will become even more noticeable. The Jamaica Public Service Co.Ltd. and Jamaica Telephone Co. Ltd. should, therefore, be invited to participate in the Falmouth Restoration Project and clear up this unsightly tangle of wires. Ideally, all wires should be run underground.

CONCLUSION

FALMOUTH is in a key location on the main north coast road, a focal point, where visitors would naturally feel inclined to stop and explore a remarkable Georgian town. This first stop will give them an idea of the richness of Jamaica's heritage, and encourage them to explore further, moving out into the countryside on the *Heritage Trail*.

We have proposed, therefore, a range of simple initiatives none of which involve substantial expenditure in the first year or two. If the right climate of enthusiasm is to be created, it is vital that these ideas are implemented together, at one and the same time – that is, all initiatives should be synchronized.

As a key initiative, the Trelawny Parish Council, at little cost, could smarten up the open spaces in its control. A striking contrast already exists between the grass around the court house, (left) seen here still littered with debris from Hurricane Gilbert over a year before, and the well tended war memorial (above) complete with trim grass and oleanders. The post office and the police post in Market Street, like the court house are public buildings where an initial facelift will transform the street scene.

Falmouth post office on Market Street.

28

- Funds must be made available for the first three years of the Grant Scheme and this would be used to provide significant incentives to each approved project.
- A Jamaican architect should begin to hold regular sessions on spot, to encourage and assist applicants as soon as the grant scheme is made available.
- A much-publicised Award Scheme for the best restoration project should be initiated. This will require a small cash sum as a prize, and the provision of a plaque to be displayed on the house. This will create a major incentive among residents.
- A dramatic clean-up of the streets and a planting programme for streets and shared spaces must coincide with the above initiatives.
- A general blaze of publicity accompanied by last, but not least, a clear understanding that the Jamaica National Heritage Trust will use its powers to take action against people who build or make additions without its consent, and adversely affect the whole project.
- Additional sums must be made available for publicity, advice, cleaning and landscaping.

A 25% incentive would lead to significant investment and to a transformation of the townscape while improving the town's economic prospects substantially.

An illustration of the iron bridge that was 'recently erected across the Martha Brae River, near Falmouth, Jamaica' from the Illustrated London News, page 564 dated Nov. 8, 1851.
Courtesy Mr and Mrs Eusebio Perez.

An example of a classic well proportioned house in urgent need of incentives.

A cottage in Queen Street. The Trelawny Parish Council should undertake an extensive planting scheme. Colonial prints of Falmouth show luxuriant plants in the streets and gardens. The parish should, therefore, establish a nursery where people could purchase, cheaply, traditional plants and shrubs. This cottage shows the colour and greenery which once abounded.

JAMAICAN
GREAT
HOUSES

3

ROARING RIVER GREAT HOUSE

ROARING RIVER great house, with rooms furnished to give people an insight into life in a great house would be particularly appropriate as a tourist attraction. This great house is spectacularly sited and little more than 20 minutes drive from the busy tourist town of Ocho Rios. More than 200,000 cruise ship passengers disembark at Ocho Rios annually, and most of them visit nearby Dunn's River Falls.

Roaring River house should become a large restaurant capable of catering to the cruise trade throughout the day. There could be a first-class restaurant in part of the building but a substantial part should be equipped as a more economical restaurant where an abundance of local fish, barbecued meats, vegetables and fruits is served. This restaurant could operate partly or wholly as a buffet, taking the opportunity to display Jamaican food for visitors, in contrast to most hotels which offer a predominantly international cuisine. We fortunately had the opportunity of sampling genuine Jamaican meals in private houses and feel that others, at all spending levels, would like to sample more Jamaican cooking and produce.

We suggest that at Roaring River, there should be a few rooms to let, in the way that restaurants in France often have a small number of rooms, so that the place always has a lived-in atmosphere. The main purpose of the proposal is to provide a very colourful place in which to eat.

Externally, Roaring River is ideal for such use as a visitor attraction and its large shady verandah is perfect for bars. It formerly had a wonderful garden. This should be restored and replanted with a wide range of tropical flowers and shrubs. Most visitors from Europe and North America will not have seen many of these and a good garden will be an added attraction. Planting should be done with a view to attracting humming birds, butterflies, etc.

One feature which has proved very popular in various English locations is a butterfly house. Jamaica has some remarkable butterflies including some very large ones that visitors would find most interesting. We also noted, while at Hope Zoo in Kingston, that a number of the island's butterflies were in danger, notably *Papilio homerus* (giant swallowtail) unique to Jamaica and which is under threat of extinction.

The Moneague Tavern in the Parish of St. Ann by Adolphe Duperly c. 1844. Being well maintained by its owner. This building is in good condition and can still be seen from the main road between Spanish Town and Ocho Rios as depicted in Duperly's lithograph.

NB *Colour photos by Marcus Binney*

31

Devon House in Kingston is an obvious model for what is being suggested. The nineteenth century mansion shows just how attractive and popular a well restored historic house, surrounded by green and well-tended gardens, can be. The attraction of Devon House is not just the show-rooms, with their antique furniture and restored decoration, but also the restaurants serving Jamaican food and especially the excellent shops selling high quality Jamaican wares.

It may be argued that Devon House is the centre of a highly populous area, while Roaring River is 20 minutes journey from Ocho Rios, but Ocho Rios has a captive tourist market consisting not only of people on cruise ships, but also from many of the island's major hotels in the area. In addition, the coast around Ocho Rios is increasingly filled with luxury villas and apartments, many for rent and quite a number belonging to overseas visitors who would appreciate an attractive restaurant, with fine views and some good shops attached.

An aerial view of Roaring River Estate in 1970.
PHOTO: Jack Tyndale-Biscoe

Roaring River, St. Ann was formerly the home of the Brownlow family. The garden could be a wonderfully colourful place to eat, while broad shady verandahs would be perfect for bars and comfortable chairs.

Roaring River, St. Ann showing the damage done by Hurricane Gilbert. Both the house and grounds have enormous potential for visitors but will always have an uncertain future if let on short term leases.

NB : There is also a Roaring River estate in the Parish of Westmoreland.

Minard Great House, St. Ann. An example of a fine 18th century plantation house in urgent need of repairs.

Minard, St. Ann formerly belonged to the Wimborne family. The main rooms should be furnished in period style with a restaurant opening onto the hall of 'worthies'.

MINARD GREAT HOUSE

MINARD itself is an excellent and engaging example of an eighteenth century great house. It was owned for a time by an Irishman, Hamilton Brown. A colourful and controversial character, Brown was also the founder of nearby Brown's Town. The later addition to the side of the main structure is probably mid-nineteenth century. Being further from the coast road than the other houses in our study, Minard is not suitable for a restaurant only. There should be other attractions.

At the centre of the estate there must be a number of different things to do and see so that visitors can easily spend a whole day entirely absorbed, and learning a great deal about Jamaica.

Since the property is further inland from the main tourist route than the other two houses in this study, there should be a reasonable amount of good holiday accommodation. Any new building, however, must not be sited in the main complex, but on lower ground to the west. The style should be that of a single storey estate building such as the range at the back of Minard itself or the coach house at Vale Royal, Trelawny.

The main rooms should be furnished as a showhouse with two rooms operating as a first-class restaurant. The kitchens, which today need to be on the same level, would be housed in the existing extension on the eastern end of the house. On the ground floor there should be a cheaper, more popular restaurant, like that proposed for Roaring River, with tables under the arcade.

A first floor room at Minard that could be attractively furnished as a restaurant or dining room.

The ground floor at Minard could be adapted as a larger buffet-restaurant, serving traditional Jamaican food, with tables under the arcade.

The gardens should be traditionally planted with a colourful range of local flowers and shrubs, making a further attraction for visitors.

New Hope, the former Resident Magistrate's house, half a mile from Minard on the same property, should be restored and used as a small museum with different rooms displaying various periods of the island's history. The main room should be furnished to show how the house would have looked around the year 1800.

The museum rooms should illustrate the various types of plantations and the way that they operated, continuing the story of the present, showing modern production of sugar cane, bananas, citrus fruits and coffee, with a glimpse of some of Jamaica's newest export earners, including reggae and tourism. All the principal export companies would be allowed to display their production cycle, in exchange for a contribution to the costs of the museum.

The surrounding garden which retains fine trees could be quickly brought back into good condition.

A view of the outbuilding at the back of Minard house. Any new buildings should be discreetly placed to the west and could be single-storeyed and similar in character to the service buildings often found at great houses like Minard.

New Hope, on the Minard estate in St. Ann, formerly the seat of the Resident Magistrate. Here a small house museum is proposed conveying the life and household of Jamaica's professional class around 1800.

SEVILLE GREAT HOUSE

T HIS IS a third great house, already in public hands, which is in a key location on the main north coast tourist route. As Seville immediately adjoins the main road, it will be one of those places, like Falmouth, which could introduce the passer-by to Jamaica's Heritage.

At present, it is opened in a very low-key way. The buildings consist of the great house, itself in good condition, an overseer's house, now abandoned and vandalized, and the remains of a water-driven sugar factory complex. As at Roaring River and Minard, there should be a restaurant facility and buffet, catering for people on the *Heritage Trail*. The overseer's house is the perfect size for a small restaurant which should, principally, serve Jamaican food.

The sugar mill itself should be partially restored, with the wheel operating as at Tryall in Hanover, and a room either in the overseer's house or in one of the adjoining buildings, explaining the process and workings of a sugar factory of this period with diagrams, photographs and illustrations of other mills.

Again, the garden around the house could be made much more interesting and attractive. At present, the average visitor will take no more than five minutes to stroll around the outside of the house and leave without any idea of the trees and plants that would have been found on an estate.

Visible from the main north coast road , the great house at Seville in St Ann is at present open in a low-key way. It should become a focal point on the proposed Jamaica Heritage Trail. If the gardens were more interestingly planted with local flowers and shrubs people would spend a much longer time visiting at the house. The patent for Seville Estate was granted in 1674 to Captain Richard Heming, who came with the Cromwellian forces in 1655. The present house was built over existing foundations by his grandson in 1745.

The overseer's house at Seville, now in an almost derelict state, is the perfect size for a restaurant serving good Jamaican food.

Just below the overseer's house is the remains of the old water wheel! and sugar works.

OTHER GREAT HOUSES.

AS WELL as visiting individual show houses, many people enjoy stopping off briefly at a number of houses, looking round the outside and taking a few photographs. In the course of two or three hours they can see five or six houses. We propose that there should be a number of heritage routes, marked on all tourist maps and signposted with special signs and symbols. One of the aims would be to take people off the main coastal route and bring them into the countryside.

A good precedent for this exists in the castles and manor-houses programme launched by the Danish Tourist Board a few years ago. Like Jamaica, Denmark has many historic houses but few of them were open to the public. Realising that owners could not be expected to go to the effort and expense of full-scale opening, the Danish Tourist Board set up a system whereby houses were accessible in varying degrees. In some cases the houses were quite simple, visible from the road, but nonetheless beautiful and striking enough to make it worthwhile to get out of the car and take a photograph. At others, visitors could stroll along a stretch of the road and see rather more. In some, the gardens and immediate surroundings of the house were accessible for a small payment.

In Jamaica, at every house visited, we found the owners or occupants very friendly and welcoming. We believe that a simple scheme on the Danish lines could be organised; for example, on the Longpond Estate to the south of Duncans in Trelawny which the Government owns and which is approximately 18,000 acres in size. On it are several great houses, such as Hyde Hall, Kinloss, Etingdon, Steerfield, Cambridge, Oxford, Georgia and Swanswick. Hyde Hall, with the picturesque remains of a stone windmill nearby, is a particularly attractive and photogenic house and would be a suitable stopping point on the *Heritage Trail.*

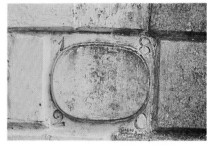

Detail of 1820 datestone on right front of Hyde Hall great house.

Hyde Hall, Trelawny. This is one of a number of great houses and associated sugar factories on the Longpond Estate which are readily visible and accessible from the passing public road. Many visitors would be delighted simply to stop and take a photograph.

The great houses are individual in character, invariably with interesting detail. At Hyde Hall notice the impressive arcade which runs back right under the house.

Near the house should be a plaque of the kind erected elsewhere by the Jamaica National Heritage Trust, explaining briefly the history of the building. While talking to the chairman of the Longpond Estate we were shown an interesting report by an industrial archaeologist. It illustrated a series of historical industrial buildings and structures on the estate which, by themselves, could form an absorbing day's sightseeing. A system of information plaques along the lines proposed could, we believe, be introduced quite quickly, easily and cheaply, not only on Government properties, but also on a number of private properties along these routes.

Montpelier in St. James, south of Montego Bay, was also visited. Although there is clearly a building which could be preserved, it is not appropriate to do so in the first phase for three principal reasons:

- *It is not close to a principal tourist route although in pleasant countryside.*
- *It is not as spectacularly sited as many other great houses – it stands in low-lying grounds without extensive views.*
- *It is a masonry building (which is unusual) and could be mothballed for a later stage of the restoration process.*

Montpelier and Drax Hall (established 1690) are certainly restorable as monies become available. Government, however, must ensure that buildings like these with considerable future potential, are not altered or restored without the consent of the Jamaica National Heritage Trust. The Government, having shown the foresight to establish the Trust, must ensure that it has the funds to make available the necessary proper architectural advice. At the same time, however, the Trust must begin to take a stronger line in protecting the more important great houses that do survive.

Front of Great House at Drax Hall Estate established in 1690. Note fine proportions of a Jamaican version of the Georgian style of architecture still visible despite unsuitable additions over the years.
PHOTO: Francis Machin

Drax Hall in St Ann. Though decayed, it stands in a wonderful position near the sea and good Georgian features survive inside. The huge palm plantations all around it have been entirely destroyed by disease. If new development is allowed in historic sites such as this, it is imperative that the plantation house and buildings be carefully restored as focal points.

SUGAR ESTATES AND INDUSTRIAL MUSEUMS

4

THE INDUSTRIAL HERITAGE

INDUSTRIAL archaeology is now a popular subject. Industrial museums and sites are rapidly increasing in number and attracting more and more visitors every year.

The famous Old Iron Bridge at Spanish Town is one example of an industrial antique. Jamaica also has a number of fascinating places where plantation sugar works have survived. Many of these are scenically situated by a river or in windswept fields, and are architecturally distinguished. In many instances, plantation owners evidently spent more money on these sugar factories than on their great houses. After all, the factories were – in terms of bricks and mortar – the major capital asset of the owner and often the owner's long term ambition was to return to England and build or acquire a fine house there.

These industrial sites scattered across Jamaica should also be marked on the *Heritage Trail* with descriptive information similar to that at great houses. In some cases there could be an outdoor display, suitably weatherproofed and set up in part of the ruins.

It is important for visitors to understand sugar processing and the various kinds of mills involved: those driven by animals, wind or water and steam. At the Spanish Town Folk Museum there is a full scale model of an animal-drawn mill, while at Hyde Hall there are wind mills. An example of a water-wheel exists at Seville, and at Orange Valley there is a mill that was once powered by steam.

At Longpond Estate, Trelawny, which is owned by the Government, there is a series of important industrial heritage sites. Swanswick is the most intact on the estate. At Linton Park, Vale Royal and the Acadia House there are interesting remains. For example, at Vale Royal there are clearly a number of walls and platforms, surviving from the original structure. Other sites on Longpond Estate are Kinloss, Etingdon, Steerfield, Cambridge, Oxford and Georgia. Because large areas of Longpond Estate are still planted in sugar cane, the countryside is more evocative of the past, and so this part of the trail is where people are likely to want to stop and take photographs. A tour of just this area, which is very accessible from the coast road between Falmouth and Duncans, would give visitors an extraordinary insight to a part of Jamaica's history. Postcards, rum and specially labelled packets of sugar could be made available for sale. The Longpond refinery

Holland Estate (St. Thomas in the East) c. 1844 by Adolphe Duperly.

NB Colour photos by Marcus Binney

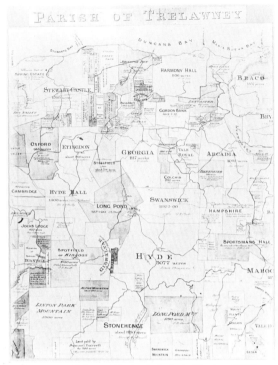

A section of Thomas Harrison's Cadastral Survey of 1878 showing some properties in Trelawny including Stewart Castle, Oxford, Cambridge, Hyde Hall, Georgia, Long Pond, Harmony Hall, Etingdon, Swanswick and Acadia.
PHOTO: Jack Tyndale Biscoe

Top Centre: a 1991 aerial photo of ruins at Barbican Estate between Maggotty and Mosquito Coves, Hanover. The windmill was in use until 1902. Note remains of round foundation.

Top right: Remains in 1991 of water wheel, aqueduct and windmill at Salem on the north coast near Runaway Bay.
PHOTOS: Jack Tyndale Biscoe

Left and above: An internal and side view of the well proportioned industrial buildings at Orange Valley in St Ann. They are still in remarkably restorable condition with surviving original steam machinery. These buildings deserve priority consideration.

Factory in Trelawny. It is desirable that people should also see a present day working factory where some of the processes still take place in Georgian buildings. After visiting the factory they could buy rum, sugar and postcards of all the plantation houses and factories on the Jamaica Heritage Trail.

Another view of the particularly fine group of sugar factory buildings at Orange Valley which are tucked in the vale below the great house.

Llandovery in St Ann is typical of many sites adjoining the tourist route where buildings could be tidied up and display panel for visitors introduced.

Orange Valley in St Ann. Spectacular scenery to be seen on the Jamaica Heritage Trail.

Orange Valley in St Ann. Until recently, the property of the Marquess of Northampton. Empty in 1990, this is another house and estate which is only a few miles from the sea and which is easily accessible to visitors.

itself contains a handsome Georgian building at its centre, complete with Palladian windows. Inside survives a remarkable array of large wooden vats, originally used for processing sugar, but now used for distilling and maturing rum.

Another easily accessible site is the remains of the sugar mill at Llandovery, in St. Ann, just east of Runaway Bay on the coast road, landmarked by a well-preserved chimney.

In a class of their own are the sugar factory works at Kenilworth, Hanover, west of Montego Bay. Kenilworth, unquestionably one of the more spectacular architectural sites in Jamaica, is not even marked on any of the main tourist maps. The first block is the sugar-boiling house and distillery; the second block is in the form of a long central room with two wings.

Architecturally, these rank with the very best Georgian industrial buildings in England, and deserve to be promoted as a high point of the *Heritage Trail*. The likelihood of the typical tourist discovering any part of this story is small, unless taken on a *Heritage Trail*. The cost of producing a good map, elegant signposts, descriptive plaques and good postcards combined with basic clearing of rubbish and overgrowth around the building is not large. Here is potential waiting to be utilized in the *Heritage Trail*.

Old steam machinery at Orange Valley, St Ann.

An aerial view of Kenilworth in 1988. Located on the Maggotty River, it was known first as Maggotty Estate and was owned by Thomas Blagrove, 1733-1755. The Blagrove family also owned Cardiff Hall in St. Ann. Today only the shells of the industrial buildings remain beside a modern youth training camp development overlooking the coast.
PHOTO: Jack Tyndale Biscoe

Front and side views of Kenilworth in Hanover. The grandest sugar factory on the Heritage Trail, it was as ambitious and sophisticated architecturally as virtually any contemporary mill in England. The ruins are well preserved but a small display for visitors is needed showing how the complex worked with a description of sugar processing from the plantation to the wharf. These handsome buildings were erected by the benevolent Blagrove family which had been in Jamaica since the British Conquest. They were best known for kindness to their slaves – the master craftsmen who would have constructed all their buildings.

A section of Thomas Harrison's Cadastral Survey of 1878 showing some properties in St. Ann including Bengal, Home Castle, Dornock Pen (where the Rio Bueno rises) , Hopewell, Dumbarton, Minard, New Hope and Orange Valley. The boundary between St Ann and Trelawny is the Rio Bueno River. See Page 80 for note on Stewart Town which is barely discernible in the extreme left hand corner of the map.
PHOTO: Jack Tyndale Biscoe

*Photograph of Seville Estate, c. 1890
showing old sugar works and cattle pens.
PHOTO: Jamaica Archives courtesy Allan Keeling.*

Wherever new development is permitted, it is crucial that any surviving elements of historic architecture are restored and adapted as part of the project. For example, if building is allowed around Drax Hall near Llandovery to the west of Ocho Rios, it must be on condition that the great house becomes a focal point which visitors and Jamaicans alike can visit and enjoy. Drax Hall is one of the estates where large plantations of coconut palms have died: any new development must be accompanied by extensive tree planting.

*The derelict sugar works and stone ruins of old wheel house with water wheel still intact at Drax Hall 1991. Planned new development must include preservation of these historic landmarks.
PHOTO: Jack Tyndale Biscoe*

The remains of the water-driven sugar mill and factory at Seville in St. Ann should be stabilized and a small explanatory display introduced.

Hyde Hall in Trelawny has one of the best and most accessible examples of the remains of a wind-driven sugar mill.

OTHER HISTORIC AREAS

5

PORT ROYAL

THE HISTORY of Port Royal has been the subject of many feasibility studies, books and published papers. Port Royal was prized first by the Spanish as an ideal location to careen their ships. When the English captured Jamaica in 1655 they recognised the strategic military significance of Port Royal and built a total of six forts making it one of the most heavily defended towns in the NewWorld. It remained an important naval station for two-and-a-half centuries and was the intermittent home of many famous British admirals.

Port Royal is popularly remembered as 'the wickedest city in the world', a reputation it held for some three decades. It was also the richest city as a result of the notorious exploits of the buccaneers who plundered Spanish settlements and attacked ships, relieving them of rich booty which they took back to Port Royal for auction to the highest bidder. The mini-city, with a population of 8000 persons and with some 2000 buildings jammed onto its tiny perch, was a sophisticated bustling 'metropolis' with a multitude of taverns and shops, silver and goldsmiths, warehouses and two prisons. In addition to two Anglican churches, there was a Presbyterian church, a Quaker meeting house, a Roman Catholic chapel and a Jewish synagogue. Despite such a strong religious presence, carousing, drunkenness, gambling and duels were rife.

It was at midday on 7 June 1692 that a massive earthquake rocked Jamaica causing two-thirds of Port Royal to slide beneath the sea. Less than one-tenth of the buildings were left standing and over 2000 souls lost their lives as a result of the disaster.

Since the great earthquake the story of the 'sunken city' of Port Royal has fascinated people all over the world and romantic ideas of retribution and sunken treasure have lived on to tantalise many a diver and developer.

As a result of several studies (including one by UNESCO in 1986) plans are presently afoot under the aegis of the Urban Development Corporation (UDC) in collaboration with Tourism Action Plan (TAP) for a projected development within the parameters of the Jamaica National Heritage Trust. This plan includes the continuing work of several overseas institutions of Anthropology and Nautical Archaeology working with Jamaican

A view of King's House in Spanish Town c. 1844 by Adolphe Duperly. Built c. 1761, since destruction by fire in 1925, only the shell of the facade facing the famous square is left standing.

archaeologists who, for several years, have been methodically investigating the underwater site and seeing to the conservation of all artifacts.

New information is therefore continually available for international scholars to study with regard to customs, lifestyles, trade interaction and general happenings of the period, not just in Jamaica but in many parts of the seventeenth century world.

The exceptional nature of this archaeological site is best expressed by Dr D.L. Hamilton and Robyn Woodward, writing in the January/February 1984 issue of the periodical *Archaeology*: '...Port Royal belongs to one of a select group of archaeological sites which includes Pompeii and Herculaneum in Italy, and Ozette in the state of Washington. Sites such as these are unique "catastrophic" sites – sites created by some disaster that preserves the cultural features and material and the all-important archaeological context. At this type of undisturbed site, the archaeologist is not dealing with a situation where – over a long span of time – houses, shops, warehouses, churches and other buildings were constructed, added on to, fell into disrepair, were abandoned, eventually collapsed, were razed and then possibly built over. Port Royal is strikingly different. After only thirty-seven years of existence, this bustling city literally sunk into the harbour in only a matter of minutes during a severe earthquake...'

Year by year, more information is retrieved by the ongoing work of archaeologists on the land and under the sea. These findings, added to and compared with existing documentation will form the nucleus of a new history yet to be written.

Port Royal can be reconstructed gradually as self-perpetuating funds become available. It can also play a pivotal role in *The Heritage Trail* as a site which can be revisited with renewed interest as new discoveries are made.

An English broadsheet publishes news of the Port Royal earthquake which took place on 7 June 1692.
PHOTO: Institute of Nautical Archaeology courtesy British Museum Library

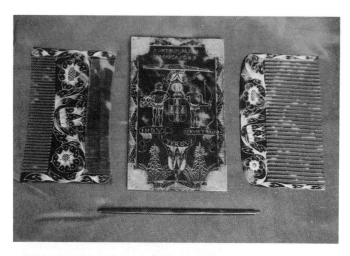

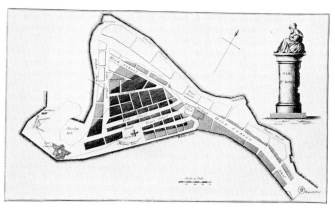

Map of Port Royal published in the Gentleman's Magazine in 1785, showing the extensive area that sank into the sea at the time of the great earthquake in 1692.
PHOTO: Kent Reid courtesy M. & V. Facey Collection

Artifacts salvaged from Port Royal seabed. Above: A sample of one of the unique tortoise shell combcases with combs embellished with silver corners, crafted at Port Royal in 1689.
Courtesy Institute of Jamaica

Left: A carved stone three-legged metate (mealing stone) with vulture head refinement, probably Taino from Central America but in use at Port Royal at time of the earthquake.

Lower left: A pair of heavily-encrusted pre1692 earthquake 'onion' bottles used for wine etc.
PHOTOS: Richard McClure Courtesy Port Royal Museum

View of Port Royal c.1744: Illustration from Edward Long's History of Jamaica.
PHOTO: Kent Reid courtesy M. & V. Facey Collection

SPANISH TOWN

THE MAIN SQUARE at Spanish Town, following the lines of the original Spanish plaza, is considered one of the finest Georgian squares in the world and is, perhaps, the grandest public space in the English speaking Caribbean. As the centre of the administrative capital of Jamaica from 1534 until 1872, the square has had special and varied historical significance for almost 500 years. It was here that the proclamation of Emancipation abolishing slavery in Jamaica was made from the steps of King's House in 1838, shortly after Queen Victoria had come to the throne of Great Britain. It is a tragedy that this building on the western side was gutted by fire in 1925. Nonetheless, its restored facade defines the ambiance and quality of the square. More recently, the court house on the southern side was burnt down in 1986. The Rodney Memorial on the northern side was erected by the grateful members of the House of Assembly after the British naval hero, Admiral George Rodney, had saved the island from capture by the French in 1782. The statue of Rodney was created by John Bacon, the most important English sculptor of the day. On the eastern side is the oldest building of the square. Until 1872 it was the House of Assembly for the colony.

Another site of historic importance is Spanish Town Cathedral, the oldest cathedral in the former British Colonies. It is officially the Anglican Cathedral of St. James, and is the parish church of St. Catherine. It stands on the site of the Franciscan Chapel of the Red Cross, built around 1525. It was one of the first ecclesiastical buildings to be established by the Spanish in the New World.

On the eastern outskirts of the town is another historic structure, the Old Iron Bridge which spans the Rio Cobre River. It was

Views of the Rodney Memorial built c. 1782 and the Old Iron Bridge (1801) in Spanish Town.
PHOTOS: Milton Williams

Aerial views of the famous Georgian Square in Spanish Town.
Above: Showing the Rodney Memorial in 1984 looking north with the House of Assembly on the east and the shell of King's House (built c. 1761 – burnt in 1925) on the west.

Left: The southern aspect showing the court house in 1960. It was destroyed by fire in 1986 and is still restorable if action is taken quickly. Note the new Jamaica Archives building under construction behind the Rodney Memorial.
PHOTOS: Jack Tyndale Biscoe

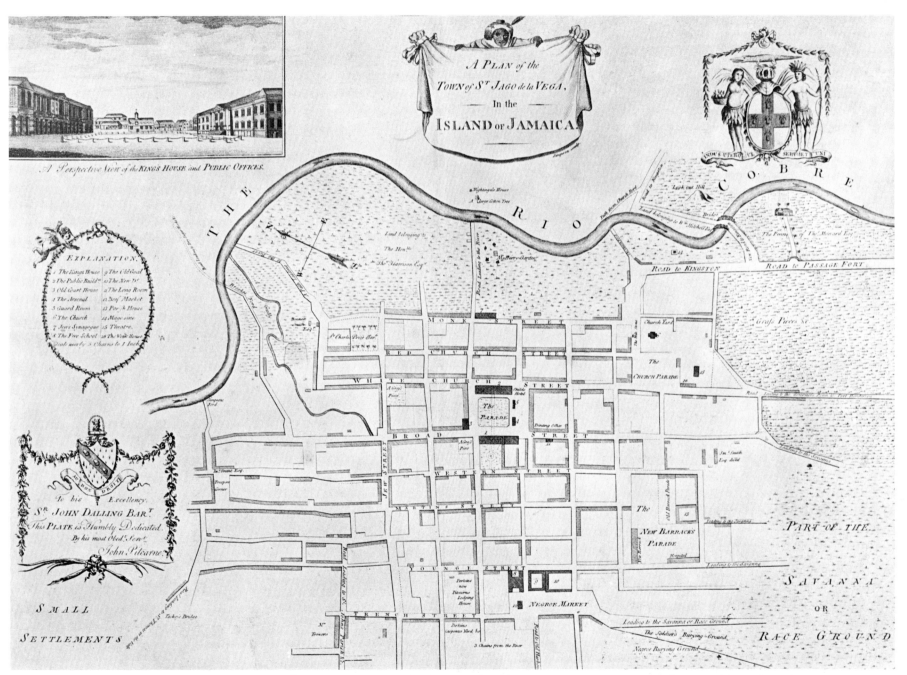

A 1786 plan of St. Jago de la Vega by John Pitcarne: This map shows the historic area of Spanish Town. Note the central square with King's House and the Public Buildings with a tunnel indicated passing between them. The Old Iron Bridge will have replaced the bridge shown at the New Road to Kingston and the present Barracks building built c. 1791 replaced the old barracks. The Rodney Memorial was built in 1782 and the court house c. 1819, completing the famous square.

PHOTO: Loaned by Raymond Brandon courtesy Jamaica Archives

49

erected in 1801 from cast-iron prefabricated segments shipped from England. It is said to have been the first cast iron bridge erected in this hemisphere and is the only one surviving.

Less than a mile up the river from the two-hundred year old bridge is the Rio Cobre Hotel. This interesting building (c. 1890) overlooking the riverfront has been from time to time both a school and a prison, but is now derelict. Serious thought must be given to the restoration of the building as a hotel once again, incorporating strategic landscaping down to the river.

A visit to Spanish Town should be one of the highlights of any stay in Jamaica but relatively few tourists visit it and even fewer stay for longer than a brief tour of the People's Museum and the Cathedral. While we have not had the opportunity to consider a restoration scheme in detail, it is clear that a project could develop on similar lines to that proposed for Falmouth.

Although Spanish Town has been given mandatory protection and is designated as an Historic District under the Jamaica National Heritage Trust Act of 1985, only the square itself seems to enjoy any form of protection whereas the actual historic area covers approximately one square mile.

Bearing all this in mind, it is gratifying to note that The Spanish Town Historic Foundation founded in 1988 by Deryck Roberts, himself a native of Spanish Town, was officially launched in 1991. Spanish Town has also been submitted to the World Heritage Committee for consideration as a World Heritage Site.

Meanwhile in 1982 the Spanish Town Task Force had proposed that the Barracks (c. 1791) be restored to house the ever-expanding Public Records and this was incorporated in the 1986 feasibility study published by UNESCO.

The Jamaica Archives, presently housed in a

building behind the Rodney Memorial, is considered one of the finest collections in this hemisphere, and is used by international scholars (such as those involved in the restoration of Colonial Williamsburg) to research material unavailable anywhere else in the world. The Public Records are presently precariously stored in inadequate locations, two adjacent to the Jamaica Archives in Spanish Town and one some eleven miles away in the city of Kingston.

At the present time, the Barracks is derelict, deteriorating and declared unsafe. It is fenced off from its surrounding parade ground which has given way to a government school. If the school cannot be relocated, it could continue to occupy the parade ground area with a modicum of rearrangement and the new repository for the Public Records could be accessed from the south facade via Nugent Street. The Barracks

Details of vernacular Jamaica-Georgian houses in Spanish Town. Note the charming detail of windows, doors, fanlights, cornice mouldings, fretwork, and bargeboards. Note also the sophisticated muted colours similar to those used at Colonial Williamsburg. The designs and colouring demonstrate an inherent astuteness of style and colour sense in people who have no formal training or experience. It is interesting to observe the subtle differences that exist between Spanish Town and other areas such as Vineyard Town in Kingston, Falmouth, Port Antonio and Black River.
PHOTOS: Deryck Roberts

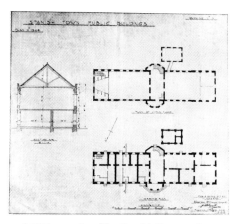

A 1951 copy plan of the Spanish Town court house built c. 1819 copied from 'Mr. Harrison's Survey 1876'. Plans such as these should always be deposited at the Jamaica Archives to assist with authentic future restoration works and general historic records. Due to the preservation of this plan, it is now possible to faithfully restore the burned out court house.
PHOTO: Courtesy Jamaica Archives

would be the perfect safe location for historic records as the windows and other orifices could be sealed off without compromising the exterior architectural integrity. It would then be an easy matter to keep this vast building as a totally air-controlled area, with room for expansion as the need arises. This action would serve two purposes: it would obviate the need for more expensive new buildings while at the same time it would preserve two international treasures for posterity – the Public Records as well as an historic building, a fine example of Caribbean architecture. The buildings vacated by the Public Records, adjacent to the Rodney Memorial, could then be used for expansion by the Jamaica Archives.

As suggested for Falmouth, the key for such a scheme must be to encourage individual house owners to repair and improve their own properties. This could be done on the basis of

substantial grants towards external repairs. While the historic area is certainly far from prosperous there is obviously money being spent on building. The need is to encourage owners to repair and construct new buildings in keeping with the historic environment of Spanish Town. Particular attention needs to be paid to fences and boundary walls. If these are trim, harmonious and freshly painted, the impression of the town will be transformed.

One or two first class hotels established within this historic area could become catalysts for the restoration and reconstruction of the entire site. It is imperative that these hotels should have excellent amenities along with suitably designed landscaping for the enhancement of the existing historic buildings.

The attraction of incorporating private sector development in a scheme of this nature is to ensure the restoration and reconstruction of historic buildings without an excessive drain on public funds. The viability of such a project would depend in large part on the *Jamaica Heritage Trail* being established and tourists beginning to spend touring holidays moving from place to place.

A few attractively appointed small hotels would also be of interest to many discerning travellers with business in the capital who want a hotel with a more distinctive and perhaps traditional character than is offered by any of the big hotels in Kingston.

A 1971 aerial view of the barracks built c. 1791. This fine building is condemned and in a state of decay but is still possible for preservation. The school could be maintained on the perimeter of the Parade and the barracks converted into a very handsome home for the Island Records.
PHOTO: Jack Tyndale Biscoe

The railway station at Spanish Town
PHOTO: Nadine Isaacs

NEW SEVILLE

SEVILLA LA NUEVA or New Seville at St. Ann's Bay was the third settlement in the New World, the first two being Santo Domingo in Hispaniola and Caperra (later abandoned), in Puerto Rico. Sevilla la Nueva was first laid out in 1509 on the order of Diego Colon, son of Christopher Columbus. He sent Don Juan de Esquivel as the island's first governor with orders to found a settlement on the site where Columbus spent a year on the island in 1503-4. Due to unhealthy conditions resulting from nearby swamps, the place did not prosper, and in 1534 the Spaniards abandoned Sevilla la Nueva and crossed the mountains to the south coast. Here they found a broad plain near a large river and built a new capital called Villa de la Vega (the town on the plains) known to the English as Spanish Town.

The UNESCO Jamaica report of 1986 includes Port Royal, Spanish Town and New Seville. This report, along with the upcoming 1992 Quincentennial Commemoration of the Encounter of Two Worlds, has put New Seville in the limelight. Columbus actually arrived in Jamaica on 5 May 1494. Nine years later, during his fourth and last voyage, he was marooned in St. Ann's Bay for over a year, which makes New Seville one of the most important *contact* sites in scholarly research. It is the only place that Columbus *lived* in the 'New World'.

The search for the two caravels known to have been scuttled by Columbus in the vicinity of St. Ann's Bay in 1503 and on which he and his 115 men lived for one year and five days, has been an ongoing project of the Institute of Nautical Archaeology in collaboration with the Government of Jamaica. Recent discoveries offer new clues: hopefully the ballast and keels from the two ships, which were lashed together, will be positively identified from the detritus thrown overboard during the year that the crew were marooned in the bay.

Anthropologically and archaeologically, New Seville and its environs offer a most exciting cross-section of history. Not only the Institute of Nautical Archaeology, but also the Spanish Government, the University of Madrid, Texas A & M University and Syracuse University as well as local archaelogists have been involved in a variety of investigations covering several different cultures in the area. Jamaica's pre-Columbian Arawak or Taino Indians were a highly civilised, peace-loving people with an advanced understanding of agriculture. Their village, Maima, near the site of New Seville has been the subject of study as a principal contact area between the Jamaican aboriginal people and the Spanish. It is recorded that some of the men who travelled with Columbus on that fateful fourth voyage (the second to Jamaica) returned six years later to remain permanently in the budding Spanish colony at Sevilla la Nueva. It was here in 1516 that the Spanish erected the first sugar mill in Jamaica. It was also the Spaniards who imported the first African slaves who arrived in the island in 1518.

It was in 1937 that excavations by a local archaeologist, Captain Charles Cotter, (1887-1977) revealed architectural remains of remarkable craftsmanship attributed to Arawaks working with Spanish artisans.

Studies of habitations in the British period include several African slave villages and the Seville great house. A series of museums and a working archaeological park are to be created with a view to having the Seville site present a comprehensive overview of the island's varied history from the advent of the Arawaks AD 600 to Independence in 1962. This would form one of the main and most easily accessible stopping points on the *Heritage Trail*.

An original pen and ink drawing dated May 1820 by James Hakewill of the coastline at St. Ann's Bay including Seville Great House taken from on board the merchant ship, the Duke of Manchester.
PHOTO: Kent Reid, courtesy of Blackwell/Paget Collection.

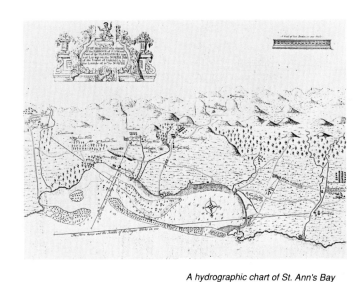

A hydrographic chart of St. Ann's Bay c. 1690 – showing very little change in the coastline. Also note the main road with the roadway to Seville Great House crossing much the way it does today.
PHOTO: Jamaica Archives courtesy Tony Goffe

Aerial view of St. Ann's Bay in foreground with the New Seville archaeological site on the middle promontory. The two caravels of Columbus were scuttled here in 1503.
PHOTO: Jack Tyndale Biscoe

To be noted in Hakewill's 1820 drawing: Columbus Cove to extreme left (A), Windsor Great House on the hill (B), Golden Spring at the top of the hill (C), on the lower right the home of the Cotter family overlooking the archaeological site at Seville (D). The centre right includes the court house (E) with Seville Great House (F) just above the works (G) and coconut trees extending to the coast lower right.

E   F G D

RIO BUENO

RIO BUENO is a small village of considerable historic interest and charm. The Georgian church overlooking the sea is already highlighted in various guidebooks as a place worthy of a special visit. As the main road runs straight through the village, the majority of tourists cruise through without stopping and the opportunity of bringing money into the local economy is largely lost.

There is no obvious place to stop or park and no clear indication of what there is to see. The first need therefore is for clear, simple signs at each end of the village announcing Rio Bueno as an 'historic Jamaica-Georgian settlement' on the lines of the brown and white signs used by the French to announce places of cultural interest.

Secondly, a simple map should be prominently displayed marking the four or five main points of interest.

Thirdly, one Georgian building needs to be restored as a demonstration project. The obvious candidate is the large warehouse on the south side of the road in the middle of the village. Though much neglected, this is an unusual and impressive building with an open verandah at first floor level that could give a great deal of pleasure to visitors.

Once it is reclad in shingles, its sweeping roofs would be picturesque and eye-catching. The original detail such as the bargeboards and the railings of the outdoor staircase must be retained, recorded and replaced where possible, in replica. Internally, the main space is large and fine. The roof timbers suitably restored, exposed and lit would look very handsome.

The warehouse is too large simply to be a museum or show place. The ideal use would be a mixture of small shops and a simple restaurant. The shops should be on the ground floor, the restaurant in the large space on the first floor. A small exhibition on the history of

Rio Bueno, Trelawny in 1990. Columbus anchored his ships here for three days after touching at St Ann's Bay on his first arrival in Jamaica, May 5, 1494. Rio Bueno Harbour is the deepest harbour in the island.
PHOTO: Jack Tyndale Biscoe

A Rio Bueno waterfront building in 1979. Note Baptist church on hill over the roof and the warehouse building across the road on right.
PHOTO: Wendy van Barneveld

Two views of the warehouse in Rio Bueno in need of urgent preservation as a suitable pilot project. Note clerestory at third floor which would be suitable for an artist in residence with a mixture of small shops, simple restaurant and a mini-museum of Rio Bueno on the lower floor.
PHOTOS: Marcus Binney

Above: St Mark's Anglican Church (1883) and remains of Fort Dundas established in 1778 at Rio Bueno. The church has been recently singled out for assistance by a benefactor.

Below: Aerial view of Rio Bueno in 1983. Note how Fort Dundas is hidden from the main road by a Government school. The fort should be cleaned up and preserved as an historic attraction with low key fencing and landscaping with salt resistant planting to protect the site from being used as a playground.
PHOTOS: Jack Tyndale Biscoe

the town could be incorporated, including its Fort Dundas which dates from 1778 and details of the interesting river and unusual bridge (completed in 1789) which gives the town its name. In the 1830s, William Knibb, the famous Baptist missionary, baptised converts at Dornoch Riverhead, where the river rises.

One good tourist facility of this kind, finished to a high standard, would provide a point where tourists could stop for a drink or a meal, spending anything from half an hour to three hours in Rio Bueno. As the approach to the restaurant would be past the shops, most tourists would make a purchase of some kind.

Virtually every small town in California now boasts a restored mill with shops and a restaurant, providing a focal point for visitors. The warehouse at Rio Bueno, carefully restored, with attention to detail, would quickly become not only a stopping point but an actual focal point for outings for tourists within a radius of 20 miles. Kidd's *Views of Jamaica* includes an excellent record of the state of Rio Bueno c. 1835, which would be an appropriate guide in the restoration of several other worthy buildings as well.

Rio Bueno in 1835 as depicted by J. B. Kidd. Rio Bueno could be restored as a model for other small historic towns. Note Baptist Church, top of the hill on left rebuilt after being burnt in 1832 in the aftermath of the definitive slave rebellion.
Courtesy National Library of Jamaica.

AN ABUNDANT LEGACY

THERE IS hardly a corner in Jamaica which does not have a story to be told. The *Heritage Trail* is a good way to retrieve some of the past before it is completely lost to future generations.

Significant villages and hamlets, if strategically selected and dealt with as suggested for Rio Bueno, could create a chain of points of interest with suitably arranged amenities to satisfy all tastes and pocketbooks. As with the Michelin Guide maps, a system of symbols would indicate what is to be seen, what is available and at what degree of comfort and cost, with the distances and time factors involved clearly defined.

Whether the individual's interest is nature, scuba diving, historic architecture, mountain climbing or documenting lighthouses, Jamaica is possessed of the legacy of a variety of features in abundance islandwide.

Folly Point Lighthouse,
built 1888, East Harbour,
Port Antonio, in Portland.
PHOTO: Alan R. Facey

MINERAL SPRINGS

Many natural springs with proven curative properties can be found such as those at Bath in St Thomas, Rockfort in Kingston, Milk River in Clarendon, Black River in St Elizabeth and Sans Souci in St Mary. Rafting is conducted on the Rio Grande, Martha Brae and White Rivers, with other associated fresh-water pleasures which include Dunn's River Falls, Blue Lagoon, Reich Falls on the Drivers River, Cane River Falls, YS Falls and a Black River boat trip where birds and crocodiles in the wild are invariably seen.

The little-known falls on the YS River near Middle
Quarters and the famous Bamboo Walk in
St Elizabeth. Photo c. 1890 with five gentlemen
wading in full European regalia minus footwear.
PHOTO: Jamaica Archives courtesy Allan Keeling

BLUEFIELDS (ORISTAN)

In the county of Cornwall in the West, from Alligator Pond past Treasure Beach and Black River to Savanna-la-Mar, on the south coast of St. Elizabeth and Westmoreland, extends some of the least known and best preserved parts of the island. At Bluefields is the site of Oristan which, after Seville, is the oldest settlement in Jamaica, established by the Spanish in the early 1530s. This area is particularly rich in natural flora and fauna as well as being steeped in history from the time of the Arawaks.

Paradoxically, the Bluefields area is also one of the most ecologically fragile of areas and any planned development has to be considered with the greatest discretion and specific understanding of its natural as well as archaeological treasures.

Bluefields in Westmoreland: stream after
flood rains in 1979. Note pipe and remains
of road demonstrating unadvised man-made
interference with nature which has invited
erosion and loss of precious top soil.
PHOTO: George Proctor courtesy
Natural History Society of Jamaica

Bluefields Bay from the air in 1990. It is one
of the most historic areas in the island. In
1670, buccaneer Henry Morgan sailed from
this bay to sack Panama. Naturalist Philip
Henry Gosse spent a year and a half here
documenting the flora and fauna in 1844-5.
PHOTO: Jack Tyndale Biscoe

BLACK RIVER AND SAVANNA–LA–MAR

From the time of the Spanish, Black River and Savanna-la-Mar were important shipping ports. Later they became cosmopolitan port towns and today some very fine architectural examples are still to be found. These could be restored or rebuilt. During the Spanish period mahogany and 'chocolata' (cocoa) were the mainstays. After 1715, logwood dye became a most important export product. Nearby Frome Estate on the Cabaritta River is among the largest and most picturesque of the oldest Jamaican working sugar plantations still in existence.

The main street in Black River, capital of St. Elizabeth, c. 1890. Up to the 1930s, the Black River Spa was a favourite watering place. Several impressive wood houses remain in precarious condition and should be documented for reconstruction.
PHOTO: Jamaica Archives courtesy Allan Keeling.

The plateau with lighthouse at 1,600 ft (480 m) known as Lover's Leap, where the Santa Cruz Mountains meet the sea in St. Elizabeth. Beyond are Alligator Pond, Old Woman's Point and Milk River.
PHOTO: Jack Tyndale Biscoe

Rhizophora mangle or Red mangroves in the Broad River, a tributary of the lower Black River. Mangroves are important as nurseries being a haven for breeding fish below water and nesting birds above and must be protected from uninhibited destruction by development projects, charcoal burning or felling for timber.
PHOTO: Ann Haynes-Sutton

Great George Street, Savanna-la-Mar, capital of Westmorland, c. 1890. Originally a Spanish port, the British founded the existing town in 1730 and built a fort at the end of this grand street.
PHOTO: Jamaica Archives courtesy Allan Keeling

A beautiful derelict old church probably dating from the 1600s at Rocky Point, Clarendon
PHOTO: Wendy van Barneveld

Black River Mangroves: The Black River is the longest river in Jamaica and is fed by many tributaries forming part of the Great Morass. The river is partially navigable and nature safari boat trips are a great attraction.
PHOTO: Ann Haynes-Sutton

LACOVIA AND THE SOUTH AREAS

On the fringe of the Black River Morass, Jamaica's largest natural wetland, is the hardly remembered, once thriving town of Lacovia founded c. 1530s. It was one of the oldest communities of secret Jews in the New World at the time when Sephardic Jews were fleeing religious persecution and the Spanish Inquisition.

Conocarpus erectus or Button Mangrove here shown as a natural giant bonsai. This noble gnarled tree has endured many a stormy sea at Heron's Reef near Treasure Beach in St. Elizabeth.
PHOTO: George Proctor, courtesy Natural History Society of Jamaica

Part of the Seven Mile Beach at Negril at the westernmost point of the island of Jamaica.
PHOTO: Jack Tyndale Biscoe

Today at Negril the beaches are being exploited for tourism purposes. There is an urgent need for precautions to be taken to modify future development with more emphasis being placed on the natural environment and less on sophisticated guest accommodation.

Between Negril and Lucea, there are many historic bays and coves, including Orange Bay, Green Island, Davis Cove, and Cousins Cove.

The town of Lucea, capital of the parish of Hanover, has its Fort Charlotte, the Old Jail, the Anglican Church, and an historic Court House with a clock tower. The recently formed Hanover Historical Society has, with the assistance of Tourism Action Plan and the Jamaica Attractions Development Company, done an excellent job of restoring the Old Jail.

Between the towns of Lucea and Montego Bay is Mosquito Cove, a designated hurricane anchorage, and the nearby grand ruins of Barbican and Kenilworth Estates. Properties at Tryall and Round Hill, now elegant resorts, were once important sugar plantations.

The town of Lucea, c. 1890 at Lucea Harbour in the parish of Hanover.
PHOTO: Jamaica Archives courtesy Allan Keeling

Fort Charlotte at Lucea, Hanover with the handsome old Barracks presently being used by the Public Works department.
PHOTO: Jack Tyndale Biscoe

NEGRIL AND THE WEST

Negril, or Punta Negrilla in Spanish days, was frequently the scene of piracy as the outpost of renegades such as Jack Rackham alias 'Calico Jack'. With his two women pirate accomplices, Ann Bonney and Mary Read, he terrorised and plundered many a passing ship.

Royal Palm Reserve at Negril. This stand of endemic palms (Roystonea princeps) is located near the Negril River and the swamp which are protected sanctuaries for plant and animal life.
PHOTO: J. W. Dalling

A view of a bridge over the Cabaritta River in Westmoreland on the estate of William Beckford Esquire in 1778.
From an engraving by George Robertson, 1778
Courtesy National Library of Jamaica

PHOTO: L. R. Owen, courtesy Tony Goffe

Left: Troilus polytmus polytmus, or 'Doctorbird' or 'Sissors-tail': the national bird of Jamaica found only in this island. Many endemic humming bird species may be seen at the Rocklands Feeding Station (above) near Montego Bay where the 'bird woman of Anchovy' invites visitors to help feed the birds.
PHOTO: Wendy van Barneveld

58

Called 'the Bay of Good Weather' in 1494 by Christopher Columbus, Montego Bay was originally one of Spain's principal provision depots for her ships sailing to and from the Spanish Main. 'Pig's butter' or lard from wild hogs and Seville orange marmalade (to prevent scurvy) were among the main staples. Montego Bay also has strong historical associations with The Second Maroon War in 1795. The central square in the town has been renamed Sam Sharpe Square in memory of the slave-leader who led the slave-rebellion of 1831. He was tried in the Montego Bay court house and, in May 1832, was hanged in the Square, then named Charles Square. After he was declared a National Hero in 1975, a monument was also erected there in his honour. There are now plans afoot to rebuild this famous court house as a cultural centre for Western Jamaica.

Since the 1920s, the town has been an international tourist resort and today the name Montego Bay is synonymous with 'Sun and Fun' Tourism, 'Reggae Sunsplash' and romantic Rose Hall.

A 1990 aerial view of Montego Bay. Top middle right is the Sangster International Airport, the most frequently used port of entry for visitors to the island. Centre is the Bogue Islands Development with the Freeport for cruise ships, resort area, yacht club, parks, resort and industrial areas.
PHOTO: *Jack Tyndale Biscoe*

Rose Hall Great House near Montego Bay in 1970 during reconstruction – perhaps the grandest great house of the Caribbean. Originally built c. 1770, it was faithfully restored by the late T. A. L. Concannon with funding provided by a U.S. entrepreneur. Hopefully one day the semi-circular wings and rear courtyard building as well as the slave quarters will be restored. There are many lurid tales of romance and intrigue connected with Rose Hall.
PHOTO: *Jack Tyndale Biscoe*

Montego Bay c. 1890 showing court house built in 1804 and the undeveloped Bogue Islands.
PHOTO: *Jamaica Archives courtesy Allan Keeling*

The Montego Bay Court House c. 1890. This building was the scene of the trial of martyr and National Hero Samuel Sharpe who was hanged in the square in 1832. William Knibb and other missionaries were tried and acquitted here. The building burned down in the 1980s and is slated for reconstruction as a cultural centre for Western Jamaica.
PHOTO: *Jamaica Archives courtesy Allan Keeling*

OCHO RIOS

The Spanish Las Chorerras, now Ocho Rios, St Ann was a sleepy fishing village fifty years ago. Today it is a wildly expanding tourist resort town with high rise hotels and two deep-water piers. Fortunately, planning is underway to monitor future development, relocate the main road for commerce and through traffic and 'cosmetise' some of the more recent, less attractive buildings. Present developers are showing a conscious effort at spending their money with a view to aesthetics as an enhancement to their earning power and their return benefits.

Ocho Rios is a favourite area for many visitors as it boasts three elegant resort hotels as well as several new all-inclusive resorts and the gamut of accommodation from private villas and apartments to very inexpensive motel-type rooms and lodging.

Few visitors come to Ocho Rios without experiencing Dunn's River Falls on the Roaring River. The name Las Chorerras refers to the many waterfalls in the area. A ten-minute three mile (4.8 km) drive through the tree arched gorge of Fern Gully takes the traveller up 1300-odd feet (440 m) to a vista of the Walkerswood area and spectacular country drives. A special side trip, well worth the effort, traces the rapids of the White River which divides the parishes of St. Ann and St. Mary. There, in a hidden river gorge, one can discover an idyllic scene, as depicted in an 1820 print by James Hakewill, of the historic *Spanish Bridge* on the *King's Road*. This was an Arawak track, followed first by the Spanish and later by the British, which originally joined the north and south coasts.

The Bay at Ocho Rios, St. Ann in 1987 showing the new pier with two cruise ships anchored. Another two ships can be accommodated at the bauxite pier in right background which is no longer used for bauxite. The old fort built in the late 1600s was located to the right of this pier.
PHOTO: Jack Tyndale Biscoe

The 'Spanish Bridge' over the White River on the 'King's Road'; an idyllic scene from an aquatint by James Hakewill drawn in 1820.
Courtesy M. & V. Facey Collection

Laughing Waters c. 1890: one of the cataracts of the Roaring River not far from Dunn's River Falls which is a popular tourist attraction.
PHOTO: Jamaican Archives courtesy Allan Keeling

St. Ann's Bay and Port Maria are two important towns slated for restoration. They must be protected *now* from further improper development. Their churches and court houses are especially fine; the court house in Port Maria burned down in 1988 and needs urgent attention.

It was near Port Maria that Ian Fleming created James Bond at 'Goldeneye' and Noel Coward found ispiration at 'Firefly'. The latter in the late 1600s was Henry Morgan's north coast mountain top lookout.

Annotto Bay and Buff Bay also deserve special attention with interesting old churches and great houses on the properties of Agualta Vale, Gray's Inn and Iter Boreale which were once vast Arawak habitations. Both Agualta Vale and Iter Boreale were demolished by fire while uninhabited within the last twenty years.

Similar notice should be taken of Oracabessa, Orange Bay, Hope Bay and St. Margaret's Bay – all quaint little villages on the old trainline to Port Antonio. This drive is perhaps the most picturesque and dramatic coastal route in the entire island of Jamaica.

The capital of Portland, Port Antonio with its strategic twin harbours, was for the Spanish and British only a safe anchorage and a place to careen their ships. It was after the 1880s, when the banana came into its own, that Port Antonio flourished, being the principal port from which bananas were dispatched to England and to America. With the banana business came tourists who built homes and found Port Antonio one of the most romantic and unspoiled spots on the globe. The old Titchfield hotel – which burned down several times and was not rebuilt after the 1969 fire – was frequented by famous people such as Rudyard Kipling, Randolph Hearst and J. P. Morgan Jr. Many movie stars holidayed there and Errol Flynn made Port Antonio his home. His widow, former actress Patrice Wymore, lives at nearby Boston looking after her cattle property and craft development enterprises. Port Antonio has a unique quality all its own and must be allowed to retain its attraction as an unspoiled haven. It also has the reputation of being one of the finest deep-sea fishing grounds in the hemisphere.

Iter Boreale near Annotto Bay before it burnt down in 1975. Built on an Arawak midden, the original great house was once owned by Sir Thomas Modyford, Governor of Jamaica 1664-1670.
PHOTO: *Courtesy Mrs Beryl Donaldson*

The strategic twin harbours of Port Antonio overlooked by Blue Mountain Peak. The Port Antonio Blue Marlin Fishing Tournament takes place here and endorses the 'tag and release' practice now recommended.
PHOTO: *Jack Tyndale Biscoe*

The view from Morgan's 1670s lookout at 'Firefly', Sir Noel Coward's residence in Jamaica (1950-1973) where he died and is buried. Note Cabaritta Island at centre.
PHOTO: *Wendy van Barneveld*

The Port Maria court house c. 1890 destroyed by fire in 1988 and in need of restoration. Originally Arawak and Spanish habitations, the capital of St. Mary was in 1760 the site of Tacky's slave uprising.
PHOTO: *Jamaica Archives courtesy Allan Keeling*

Upstairs balcony detail of Port Antonio railway terminus built c.1890.
PHOTO: *Nadine Isaacs*

Ruins near Stokes Hall, one of the oldest existing foundations in Jamaica dating from about 1656 located in the Golden Grove area of St. Thomas. The 1841 Morant Point lighthouse is off to the right with extensive sugar cane fields on the Duckenfield Estate.
PHOTO: Jack Tyndale Biscoe

A closer view of the grand stonework at Stokes Hall.
PHOTO:
Wendy van Barneveld

Further east, Manchioneal, Golden Grove, Port Morant, Morant Bay and Yallahs deserve consideration. The Morant Point Lighthouse, cast in 1841, is the oldest in the island. Morant Bay was the scene of the tragic 1865 rebellion from which emerged two martyred National Heroes, Paul Bogle and George William Gordon, both hanged in front of the now rebuilt Morant Bay court house. The only National Heroine, 'Nanny', who was a Maroon military tactician and chieftainess during the first Maroon War, outsmarted the British in the Blue Mountains high above Morant Bay. In 1734 her mountain hideout at Old Nanny Town was eventually destroyed by Captain Stoddart and she moved her people to New Nanny Town, now Moore Town near the Rio Grande.

Portland, which receives the heaviest rainfall in the island is lush, mountainous and green and has some of the most breathtaking topography. In contrast, parts of St. Thomas, in the rain shadow of the mountains, are stony and almost arid. Behind the coast and the lowlands, the peaks of the Blue Mountains rise steeply to a spectacular 7,402 feet (2243 m).

An aerial view of Morant Bay which in 1865 was the scene of a tragic rebellion which signalled a turning point in Jamaica's history. National Heroes Paul Bogle and George William Gordon were hanged in front of the court house, over 430 citizens were killed or executed and over 1600 homes were burnt. Originally Arawak and Spanish habitations, this area is of outstanding historic interest.
PHOTO: Jack Tyndale Biscoe

Christ Church, Morant Bay, the Anglican Parish Church of St Thomas consecrated in 1865 near the site of an old church which may have originated when Morant was a Spanish settlement in the 1500s.
PHOTO: Herbie Gordon

A banana field in the Morant area c. 1890. Morant Bay and Bowden used to be important banana shipping ports. The Bowden Formation is the subject of significant palaeontologic interest and is rich in special fossils and ancient life forms.
PHOTO: Jamaica Archives courtesy Allan Keeling

A stone at Nanny Town with crudely carved inscription:
'December 1734
This town was took
By Coll Brook
and after kept
By Capt Cooke
Till July 1735'
PHOTO: Bobby Rodrigues

The Blue Mountains area was the hiding place for many maroons. It is said that a secret Maroon trail existed from Portland to the Cockpit County to facilitate messages between settlements at Accompong and Nanny Town. Runners could make the journey in three days despite the forbidding terrain.

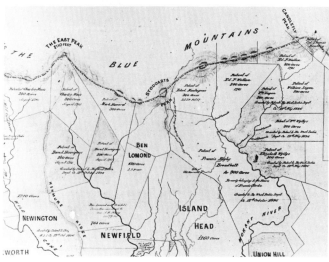

Above: An aerial aspect of part of the Blue Mountains from the St. Thomas side. On the left, the ridge is rising to the East Peak 7110 ft (2155 m) with nearby Stoddarts Peak from which descends a tributary of the Morant River. Centre Right is Candlefly Peak.

Left: Detail of the same area from the 1878 cadastral survey of Jamaica by Thomas Harrison, the Jamaican Surveyor-General of Jamaica 1862-1892. His 138 section cadastral survey of the entire island is one of the country's national treasures. It was from Stoddarts Peak that Captain Stoddart made his attack on Nanny, the Maroon Chieftainess, Jamaica's only National Heroine. Eventually in 1734 he destroyed her town in the Portland valley below. The British soldiers dragged their small cannon to this mountain top to overcome Nanny and her legendary stronghold.
PHOTOS: Jack Tyndale Biscoe

The Rio Grande in spate at a point not far from Moore Town (New Nanny Town) between the Blue Mountains and the John Crow Mountains on the eastern end of Portland and the island of Jamaica.
PHOTO: Ann Haynes-Sutton

KINGSTON

Above: An aerial aspect of Kingston Harbour – the seventh largest natural harbour in the world – looking west with the Palisadoes, airport and Port Royal on the left, Harbour View housing at eastern end and city of Kingston on the right.
PHOTO: Jack Tyndale Biscoe

Below: A drawing of Kingston Harbour and Port Royal c. 1774 from Edward Long's History of Jamaica of that date. Kingston and Port Royal once boasted eight forts and was an important British naval stronghold for two-and-a-half centuries.
Courtesy M & V Facey Collection

Kingston owes its birth to the earthquake of 1692 when survivors went across the harbour to found a new settlement at Col Barry's 'Hog Crawle'. However, it did not become the island's capital until 1872. Potentially, Kingston, with its dramatic setting between the Blue Mountains and Kingston Harbour (which is the seventh largest natural harbour in the world) is one of the most important visitor destinations in Jamaica. Kingston has many special places of interest within driving distance such as Newcastle, with access to the Blue Mountain Peak area; three botanical gardens; Dallas and the Cane River; Spanish Town; Port Royal, Hellshire and the Cays. Kingston reverberates with energy as a pulsating business centre and it is also the hub of the island's social, intellectual and artistic expression. Here is the home of the Institute of Jamaica – the country's governing cultural body – its museums, the National Library, the National Gallery, the University of the West Indies, the schools of Art, Drama, Dance and Music, the theatres and myriad private art galleries.

For the past ten years, the Kingston Restoration Company (KRC), a joint private sector/public sector, non-profit organisation with special funding from the United States Agency for International Development (USAID) and the private sector, has been blazing new trails with its revolutionary ideas and schemes with regard to the restoration of a city centre in decay. Other cities in other countries have begun to take note of the results being achieved by this restoration programme. It is the intention of Tourism Action Plan (TAP) to use the same concept in their plans for the improvement of the infrastructure for the entire island, starting with Falmouth. It is intended for these plans to incorporate the *Heritage Trail*.

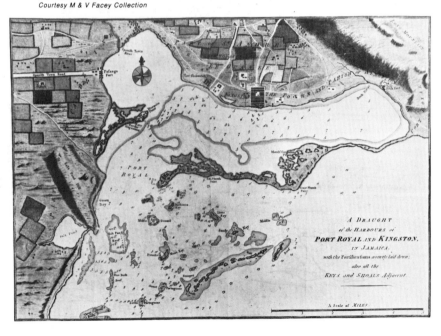

Exterior and interior views of the Kingston Railway Terminus built in 1845 and operating on a small scale today.
PHOTO: Nadine Isaacs

The Ward Theatre in downtown Kingston today. The first 'Public Theatre' in Jamaica was documented in 1682.
PHOTO: Milton Williams

Above: an aerial photograph of the city of Kingston looking south from Catherine's Peak and overlooking Newcastle. The Palisadoes and Port Royal can be seen in the far distance.

The University of the West Indies with backdrop of mountains: Catherine's Peak is at centre and Newcastle to the left, slightly below.

Left: Newcastle c. 1890 (above) and as it is today (below). Established as a military camp in 1841 at a cool altitude of 4000 ft (1212 m), this Jamaica Defence Force hill station is a place of special historic interest with a spectacular view.

AERIAL PHOTOS: Jack Tyndale Biscoe
OLD PHOTO: Jamaica Archives courtesy Allan Keeling

King Street in 1885. Note mule-driven tram cars, the Victoria market (in lower right corner) and mountains towards Newcastle in the background.

Port Royal Street c. 1890. The many pre -1907 earthquake brick buildings and delicate balconies are still in evidence. Note multiple telegraph poles lining the unpaved street.

Harbour Street c. 1890. Note the elegant building proportions, arches and columns. Has the tree been retained (at the peril of the house) for its shade or its sign-hanging ability?

East Queen Street c. 1890. Note buried cannon (muzzle down) which, before the advent of telegraph poles, would have protected the edge of the building from horse-drawn carriages turning the corner.

Harbour Street c.1890 with its scaffold tower lookout to observe ships in the harbour and spot fires. The extensive use of jalousies permitted good ventilation.

East Street c. 1890. Note gas lamps. Escaping gas was the culprit reputed to have caused the fire that burned the city of Kingston at the time of the 1907 earthquake disaster.

PHOTOS: Jamaica Archives courtesy Allan Keeling

ENVIRONMENTAL CONSERVATION

6

THE NATURAL HERITAGE

THE GROWING INTEREST in preserving and restoring historical sites is part of a more general movement which is seeking to conserve the indigenous and most distinctive elements of Jamaica's cultural and natural environment.

The uniquely beautiful and varied landscape of Jamaica is an intricate patchwork of natural and man-made elements. The magnificent and unique rain-forests of the Blue Mountains; the stunted and gnarled dry coastal forests; the strange-rooted mangrove forests and lagoons; the richly coloured coral reefs; and the man-made counterpoint of limestone woodlands and pastures of central Jamaica; the checked agricultural savannas of southern St Elizabeth; as well as the cultivated cane fields of the coastal plains: all are examples of Jamaica's rich natural legacy. In these habitats flourish untold riches of biodiversity. More species of birds (including the Doctorbird, two species of parrots and the Jamaican Tody) are endemic to the island of Jamaica than to any other comparable island worldwide.

Almost a third of Jamaica's plants are found nowhere else in the world. Today many species and their habitats are threatened by pollution and inappropriate exploitation.

Like historical buildings and sites, the natural environment often requires interpretation and restoration in order to make it attractive and accessible to visitors. A system of national parks and protected areas is necessary to ensure that the best and most typical of Jamaica's natural assets are retained for the enjoyment, appreciation and economic welfare of present and future generations. An important by-product of conservation of natural areas will be the protection and improvement of water supplies and reduction of the effects of natural disasters on coastal settlements. The private sector, guided by the government, will therefore, have a very important role to play in the establishment of protected areas.

Many of the most important and interesting historical sites and buildings of the proposed *Heritage Trail* are closely associated with areas which are of ecological importance.

A view of the court house at Bath in St. Thomas-in-the-East c. 1844 by Adolphe Duperly. Note tree specimens in the nearby Bath Botanic Gardens established in 1779, presently the oldest of five Jamaican botanical gardens founded in the island.

When historical sites can be conserved in the context of historical landscapes the overall interest to Jamaicans and to visitors will be greatly enhanced. It is important to determine the carrying capacity of natural resources and to monitor them in order to avoid either desecration or over-exploitation.

The town of Falmouth is framed by a significant wetland and some of the most spectacular coral reefs in Jamaica. Hyde Hall, Kinloss House and Gibraltar are all on the fringes of the Cockpit Country, one of Jamaica's proposed national parks, as is Windsor Great House and the Windsor Cave from which the Martha Brae River springs and flows back to the sea at Falmouth. With the development of displays, trails and other facilities, places like this could form convenient bases for interpretation and exploration of the unusual and interesting cockpit landscape and its fauna and flora. Interest from the tourism sector would help to provide an impetus for active conservation and sustainable development of this valuable area where more than 100 species of plants are rare or endangered.

Other places which are of outstanding interest and importance for ecological conservation include the Blue Mountains and John Crow Mountains (the site of Jamaica's first proposed national park); Montego Bay (the site of a marine park); the central mountains of St. Ann and adjacent parishes; Discovery Bay and environs; Black River Lower Morass; Canoe Valley; Port Royal, Hellshire and Portland Bight and Ridge; Negril; Dolphin Head and the Blue Lagoon. Of these, Black River and Port Royal are particularly rich in historical and cultural associations.

(Amazonia Collaria): *endangered yellow-billed parrots found in the Cockpit Country.*
PHOTO: Y. J. Rey-Millet

Hyla wilderi: *One of the many species of whistling frogs found only in the Cockpit area. Varieties of these tiny, rarely seen creatures are responsible for the amazing chorus heard at night in damp tropical conditions.*
PHOTO: S. Blair Hedges

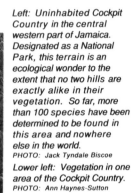

Left: Uninhabited Cockpit Country in the central western part of Jamaica. Designated as a National Park, this terrain is an ecological wonder to the extent that no two hills are exactly alike in their vegetation. So far, more than 100 species have been determined to be found in this area and nowhere else in the world.
PHOTO: Jack Tyndale Biscoe

Lower left: Vegetation in one area of the Cockpit Country.
PHOTO: Ann Haynes-Sutton

A part of the Broad River with dried vegetation and flying egrets: part of the designated national park at the Black River Lower Morass.
PHOTO: Ann Haynes-Sutton

One of the planned national parks: Royal Palm Reserve (Roystonea Princeps) at Negril.
PHOTO: Wendy van Barneveld

The Clyde River Valley looking towards Clydesdale and John Crow Peak in the Blue Mountains on the border between St. Andrew and Portland at the eastern end of the Island: part of a new designated National Park.
PHOTO: Andreas Oberli

Below: Passiflora macfadyenii *photographed along the Cane River Road. A member of the passionfruit family suitable as wild stock for interbreeding of edible fruit. Unique to Jamaica, this very rare species only occurs in a small area of the Cane River, St. Andrew.*
PHOTOS: George Proctor courtesy NHSJ

Above: The almost forgotten Cane River Falls in the Port Royal Mountains to the east of Kingston. From the early 1800s to the early 1900s this area was a renowned beauty spot for visitors and is the habitat of a very rare plant species.
PHOTO: Andreas Oberli

Spathelia sorbifolia *photographed in Clarendon, known as 'Mountain Pride', is perhaps the most unusual, spectacular and sadly romantic of Jamaica's endemic flowering trees; is rarely seen due to habitat on limestone crags. Legend tells of an Arawak princess who threw herself over a cliff at her wedding feast when her Cacique groom was poisoned by the jealous village priest. 'Mountain Pride' returns periodically in her palm-leaf skirt and crown of pink feathers to entice us from her high rock ledge. When 8-10 years old, the tree blooms briefly and dies.*
PHOTO: George Proctor courtesy Natural History Society of Jamaica

A Jamaican Hamelia, *commonly known as 'Prince Wood', photographed in Trelawny. An attractive shrub with bright gold flowers with two endemic species: this plant is related to coffee and has potential for horticulture.*
PHOTO: George Proctor courtesy NHSJ

Portlandia grandiflora *found at Stop and Think in St. Catherine between Guanaboa Vale and Watermont. The genus* Portlandia *is endemic to Jamaica and has tremendous horticultural potential because of the diverse form and colour; varieties also exist in pink, white and crimson.*
PHOTO: George Proctor courtesy NHSJ

Over 550 indigenous species of ferns are found in Jamaica. Shown here is a typical tree fern, Cyathea sp., *which grows in mountain rain forest and can attain heights over 30 ft (9 m) tall.*
PHOTO: J.W. Dalling

Environmental conservation requires consideration for the entire ecosystem, a delicate balance between climate, trees, rainfall, plant life, insects, birds, etc., none of which can exist without the other. The special areas described abound with remarkable birds and creatures which co-exist with the extraordinary and abundant plant life in Jamaica.

The internationally renowned naturalist Philip Henry Gosse (1810-1888) spent eighteen months in Jamaica in 1844-45, almost exclusively in the Bluefields area of Westmoreland. It was here that he wrote and illustrated his classic books on Jamaica's natural history, including the some 200 species of birds found in the island of which 25 species and 21 sub-species are found nowhere else on the globe.

Below: Papilio homerus. *There are 21 endemic species of butterfly in Jamaica of which the giant swallowtail, with a wing-span of 6 in (15.2 cm), is the most sought after by collectors as one of the largest species in the western hemisphere. Its main habitat is a remote part of the John Crow Mountains (left) which is relatively inaccessible.*
PHOTO: Butterfly: Eric Garraway
Mountains: Rhema Kerr, Hope Zoo

Mention must be made of the botanical gardens of Jamaica. It is notable that in an area of 4,411 sq. miles (10,830 sq. kms), five botanical gardens were established, prior to the start of the twentieth century, of which four still exist. The first, founded by Hinton East c. 1750, at Spring Garden and Enfield in St. Andrew, was later abandoned. The Garden at Bath, adjacent to the famous curative hot and cold springs discovered in the 1690s, was established in 1779. This is where the first breadfruit tree seedling, straight from the ship *Bounty*, was transplanted in 1793. Bath is the oldest Botanic Garden in Jamaica but, ironically, it is also the most neglected of the several diminishing arboreta.

In 1862, Castleton Gardens, at an altitude of 500 ft (170 m) in Northern St. Andrew, was created as the principal botanical headquarters and, in 1868, Cinchona was established at 5,000 ft (1,700 m) in the heart of the Blue Mountains which rise to 7,402 ft (2,243 m). This botanical garden was started in order to cultivate the cinchona tree for commercial quinine in addition to tea for export.

The most popular botanical gardens were laid out at Hope Estate on the Liguanea Plains

At Cinchona Botanic Gardens, 5,000 ft (1,700 m) in the Blue Mountains, a finely proportioned house built c. 1870 as the residence of the then Island Botanist. It is from the bark of the cinchona tree that quinine, the remedy for malaria is extracted.
PHOTO: Andreas Oberli

An example of exotic or introduced tropical plants as can be seen at Castleton Gardens at 500 ft (170m) in the Wag Water Gorge of St. Andrew on the border of the parish of St. Mary: presently the finest botanic garden in the island of Jamaica.
PHOTO: Andreas Oberli

Aechmea paniculigera: bromeliad or wild pine, endemic to the western half of Jamaica only. This species grows on rocks as against a closely related one in the eastern part of Jamaica which only grows on tree trunks.
PHOTO: Peter Vogel

A Rock Beauty at Discovery Bay. Efforts are presently being made to protect Jamaica's reefs which are in danger of extinction if immediate care is not taken to educate people to understand the vital ecology of the sea.
PHOTO: William K. Sacco

Eichhornia crassipes or Water Hyacinth, a native of Brazil. The most unfortunate introduction of this plant now causes clogging of waterways and ponds which eventually suffocates the natural wildlife living in the system.
PHOTO: Rhema Kerr, Hope Zoo

Blossom Brand Tea was grown and packed at Ramble near Claremont in St. Ann c. 1903. Tea was introduced to Jamaica from Ceylon c. 1874 and the seedlings were nurtured at Cinchona Botanic Garden. Coffee was introduced in 1728 and planted at Temple Hall in St. Andrew.
PHOTO: Courtesy Raymond Brandon

An idyllic scene at Gut River in the Canoe Valley Park area in the Parish of Manchester. These places of natural beauty must remain protected and unspoiled.
PHOTO: Wendy van Barneveld

Wood and Water Day in 1986 at Alligator Hole River in Manchester, on the Canoe Valley Coastline. In this 5,000 odd acre naturalists' paradise, one can still encounter crocodiles and manatees. At Round Hill are some of the earliest Arawak remains.
PHOTO: Ann Haynes-Sutton

A concerted effort is being made to protect the almost extinct Jamaican iguana 'lizard' (Cyclura collei) which was prized as food by the Arawaks. Its eggs are preyed upon by the mongoose. Only a few specimens survive at Hellshire in St. Catherine.
PHOTO: Peter Vogel

Todus todus: *Jamaican Tody or 'Jamaica Robin'. This tiny emerald green bird with red throat and bill is endemic to Jamaica and builds its nest in holes in the ground.*
PHOTO: Tony Diamond courtesy Gosse Bird Club

Pseudoscops grammicus: *the Jamaican brown owl found only in Jamaica is commonly called 'patoo' and is the subject of much superstition.*
PHOTO: Rhema Kerr, Hope Zoo

Anthracothorax mango: *Jamaican mango hummingbird, endemic to Jamaica and highly prized by bird lovers for its irridescent magenta plumage.*
PHOTO: Tony Diamond courtesy The Gosse Bird Club

Columbra caribaea *or Ring-tailed Pigeon in captivity at the Hope Zoo. This gentle Jamaican endemic is endangered due to indiscriminate deforestation and the improper habits of some unprincipled sportsmen.*
PHOTO: Rhema Kerr, Hope Zoo

Herpestes auropunctatus: *A specimen of the ubiquitous mongoose at the Hope Zoo, a classic example of the unpropitious introduction of a species. In 1872 nine were imported into Jamaica from India to eliminate rats destructive to crops and then multiplied to become an islandwide pest.*
PHOTO: Rhema Kerr, Hope Zoo

Crocodylus acutus: *a survivor from the days of dinosaurs, the Jamaican crocodile – not to be confused with the alligator which it is called – features on the Jamaica Coat of Arms and has been protected as endangered by the wildlife law since 1971.*
PHOTO: Rhema Kerr, Hope Zoo

in 1881 and gained the distinction of becoming the Royal Botanic Gardens in 1953 at the time of the first visit of Queen Elizabeth II to Jamaica. The Hope Gardens incorporate the Hope Zoo, which is presently being assisted by the Jersey Wildlife Preservation Trust and the Canadian International Development Agency (CIDA). Plans call for an expansion in the number of Jamaican and Caribbean species of flora and fauna held.

Apart from being a place of beauty, the role of the botanical garden is to see to the proper introduction of useful plant species, the development of commercial varieties, the propogation of endangered species and for scientific research and education.

In latter years all these aspects have been neglected. In 1990 the National Arboretum Foundation of Jamaica was founded with the conservation of the island's botanical gardens and endangered plant species being its main objective. This coincides with a world movement to rescue the imperilled environment. The recent visit of Professor Vernon Heywood, Chief Scientist, Plant Conservation, World Conservation Union (IUCN) and Director, Botanic Gardens Conservation Secretariat at Kew in Britain, is an indication of the perceived importance worldwide of the Botanic Gardens of Jamaica.

It goes without saying that the four Botanic Gardens must become part of the *Heritage Trail.* It is also pertinent to suggest that an *Arawak Nature Trail* be conceived to cater to the naturalists and those interested in the areas in Jamaica least affected by civilisation. The new crop of naturalist groups such as the revived Natural History Society of Jamaica (NASJ) and the more recently founded Jamaica Conservation and Development Trust (JCDT) is heartening and shows a providential infusion of new interest in the vital subject of conservation.

THE CONTRIBUTION OF PRIVATE ENTERPRISE

7

THE HERITAGE RESPONSIBILITY

THE PRIVATE SECTOR has already indicated its interest in the restoration of historic buildings for tourism purposes. An excellent example is the shop, gallery and restaurant at Harmony Hall, near Ocho Rios, which have been established in a charmingly restored manse. This kind of operation could be repeated elsewhere, on or near the main coastal tourism route. The overseer's house near Seville Great House, for example, could have a similar restaurant/gallery.

The delightfully rustic hamlet of Walkerswood in St. Ann is a perfect example of how even a tiny community can improve their environment. In 1983 when the rented premises used for the post office were no longer available, the local citizens banded together and, with the help of two established farms in the area, made the necessary petitions to the authorities. They then obtained materials, and the result was a brand new post office designed and built by the citizens themselves near their community centre and playfield.

At the other end of the scale, the great house at Good Hope, Trelawny, the focal point of the best collection of Georgian buildings on any estate in Jamaica, is presently being restored by a consortium of private entrepreneurs. The new owners plan to furnish the main house appropriately and it is envisaged that all the derelict estate buildings, including the sugar factory and slave hospital will be restored.

A third example of successful private sector restoration is the restored Albert George Market in the town of Falmouth where small shops have been successfully created within an historic complex. Any new development on such lines should be included on the new tourist maps and route signs, provided it meets three simple criteria:

- *that it is of worthy standard*
- *that it contributes to the restoration of an historic building, large or small*
- *that it is accessible to the public.*

Nearly all the principal buildings in our study are owned by Central Government so there is opportunity for private sector involvement on a partnership basis in the development of these sites.

In many cases we believe that long leases, and by this we mean leases of 99 years, are the key to stimulating good quality schemes that will make a positive contribution to Jamaica's tourist industry.

A view of the court house in Kingston on an election day c. 1844 by Adolphe Duperly. Kingston is still the seat of the Government, Judicial System and Stock Exchange.

The Government should not exclusively seek the highest offer, but should find the person who contracts to produce a certain type of development. For example, as the private sector has already produced Harmony Hall, we are certain that, for a long lease, and a low purchase cost, a sympathetic private investor could be found to take on the overseer's house at Seville. The long lease would allow the Government to retain overall control of the future of the building but would make it worthwhile for the investor who must put up a substantial sum to restore, adapt and equip the building.

Private investors have proved willing to spend large sums on improvements at Good Hope, as well as the purchase price for the house with a very substantial acreage, and we think it likely that a private investor or consortium could be found to put a substantial sum of money into Roaring River in exchange for a long lease and inclusion in the *Heritage Trail*. If the *Heritage Trail* is successful, there is only a limited number of exceptional historic buildings close by. As a result, these investors will benefit substantially from the marketing programme and they would be leasing valuable properties. However, these would return at the end of 99 years lease to the Government which would then have the full benefit of all the investment put into the properties. By contrast, if the present situation continues, many of these buildings will disappear completely in the next decade and will be worth nothing.

For some sites the returns will be small; for example the proposed museum at Good Hope and the restored Barrett House in Falmouth. Individual companies or consortia would have to be found to sponsor these projects. It should be emphasized that these companies will benefit, not only from the association of their names with a particular property, but also from the kudos of contributing to what could become one of the principal tourist attractions in the entire Caribbean.

Of course, there are certain areas where funding would not come from individuals or companies and here Tourism Action Plan Limited (TAP), combined with Central Government, can unlock the door by

- *undertaking the initial investment in setting up the trail signs and exhibition areas*
- *providing well designed posters, postcards, maps, leaflets etc.*
- *initially establishing in Falmouth the grants for improvements to public areas*
- *providing architectural advice initially in Falmouth and then elsewhere.*

Many of these projects do not involve substantial sums of money. The most expensive project would be the Grant Scheme for Falmouth. In this connection, a local architect has already done a detailed report on the town's restoration and this can be used as a basis for comparison with grant schemes in England and Scotland. Sixty buildings are listed in the report as being worthy of restoration and as being especially in need of repair. If ten such buildings came up each year for grant aid, over a six year period, the town would be transformed into one of the major heritage sites in the Caribbean.

The total costs involved would be minuscule compared to amounts already being spent on promoting the island each year.

Bryan Castle in 1990, 3 miles (5 km) from Rio Bueno. This was built c. 1730 by the Edwards family and completed by Bryan Edwards in 1793. It was here that planter and merchant Bryan Edwards, (1743-1800) wrote 'The History, Civil and Commercial, of the British Colonies in the West Indies' (1793). This ruin is a prime candidate for restoration by private investors, possibly as a small hotel on the Heritage Trail. Superbly sited, the house was once a handsome example of many stages of Jamaica-Georgian architecture. No further alterations should be made without the consent and advice of the Jamaica National Heritage Trust.
PHOTO: Marcus Binney

Above: Bryan Castle in 1820 from an aquatint by James Hakewill.
Courtesy Facey/Boswell Trust Collection
Below: Aerial view of Bryan Castle in 1991.
PHOTO: Jack Tyndale Biscoe

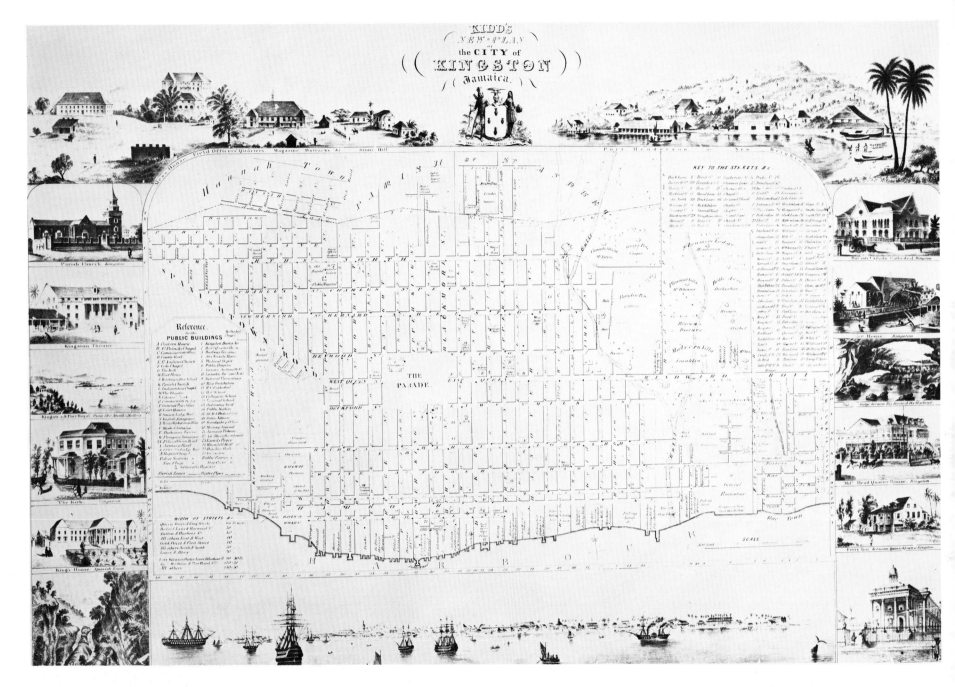

A decorative map of the city of Kingston drawn by the English artist, Joseph Bartholemew Kidd c. 1835. This map is embellished with miniature drawings of the many fine buildings that existed including the barracks at Stony Hill (top left) and Headquarters House (third from lower right side). Originally known as Hibbert House after the prominent planter, merchant and member of the Assembly, Thomas Hibbert, it was built in 1755 as part of a wager with three other wealthy Kingston merchants as to who could build the finest house. Later, it was here that Jamaica's Legislature met for nearly 100 years. Since 1983, it has been the home of the Jamaica National Heritage Trust. Unfortunately, many of these buildings, especially those of brick, were destroyed in the earthquake of 1907.

PHOTO: Courtesy National Library of Jamaica

ROADS AND ROUTES

8

THE JAMAICA HERITAGE TRAIL

OUR OVERALL PLAN is that the *Jamaica Heritage Trail* should eventually be expanded to encompass the entire island of Jamaica linking all significant villages and landmarks for the enjoyment of Jamaicans and visitors alike. Each segment should stand on its own, so that specific tours and areas can be easily mapped for exploration by persons themselves or be recommended as official tours depending on the individual's requirements.

Today the visitor to Jamaica, if he leaves his hotel complex at all, tends to ply back and forth along the main coast road from Montego Bay to Ocho Rios where many stretches of coastline have been, in effect, mugged by tourism, and have suffered from sporadic uncontrolled development.

He will probably not appreciate that he is seeing only a tiny portion of an island which has some of the most beautiful unspoilt scenery in the world. It is vital, therefore, that further damaging development of this kind is prevented and that positive measures are taken to reduce the impact of recent unsympathetic development.

The key to this is landscaping and tree planting, or in more built up areas, the introduction of shrubs such as oleanders and hibiscus in addition, whenever possible, to hardy endemic species such as the scarlet flowered cordia tree and the euphorbias. Old prints show that much of the coastal road was lined with tall palms of exceptional beauty.

No significant effort has been made to plant out or screen the worst eyesores on this very important route along the north coast, or to encourage new farming enterprise on what appears to be large areas of derelict agricultural land (notably the numerous coconut plantations killed by disease which has left a landscape of lifeless trunks).

The reintroduction of lines or avenues of disease-resistant palms would make much of the road memorably attractive and photogenic, an important consideration for tourism purposes. Some good planting of flowering shrubs has been done, however, on the approaches to the new round-about west of St. Ann's Bay on the north coast.

The Ferry Inn on the Spanish Town Road near Kingston c. 1844 by Adolphe Duperly. This building could still be salvaged though at considerable expense which would have to include heavy landscaping to camouflage the unattractive adjacent developments. Being on the main route out of Kingston, it could be very successful in the same role it played over 150 years ago.

Even more urgent is the need to protect all stretches of the road which retain their rural or scenic character. For example between St. Ann's Bay and Runaway Bay there is a particularly attractive and unspoilt stretch of country road running past Llandovery farms. No new buildings visible from the road should be allowed here or on similar stretches of attractive road. It is also essential that new buildings are concentrated in certain areas so that some sections of the coastal route retain their unspoilt country image . Where new buildings are located, Parish Councils must make more effort to encourage – indeed only allow – new buildings which, while they may be constructed in a modern manner, are appropriately designed in Jamaican traditional style. A number of local architects are already responding in this way with good results; this must be encouraged.

It is also suggested that scenic stretches of road should be marked on tourist maps. The obvious model is the Michelin maps of Europe on which pretty roads with a green edging are indicated *parcours picturesque* .

Cardiff Hall near Runaway Bay, St Ann. Owned in the 1700s and 1800s by the Blagrove family, it is still in good condition.
PHOTO: Jack Tyndale Biscoe

Devon House, Kingston: the most successful, restored 19th century great house with museums, shops, restaurants and landscaped gardens.
PHOTO: Milton Williams

Scenic routes should be designated inland as well as along the coast with a view to encouraging people to explore Jamaica's countryside. In particular we suggest a signposted *Plantation* route taking people inland past plantation houses and sugar factories. Picturesque routes such as those through Fern Gully near Ocho Rios and Bamboo Walk near Lacovia in St Elizabeth take the visitor through rich, well farmed country and present a totally different picture of the island from many stretches of the coastal route. For example, there is a very rewarding drive south from Duncans, past Vale Royal estate to Longpond refinery and then past Hyde Hall, Orange Grove and Florence Hall. Further west there is a wonderful cross-country drive from Good Hope in Trelawny to Montego Bay in St James.

These country routes have the added attraction that they take the visitor away from the heavy traffic on the coast, the trucks and the buses, and offer a much more relaxed way of travelling. It is important to indicate where the country roads are not yet paved, for while some of these roads have surfaces as good as the main coast road, others could be improved.

Good Hope, Trelawny, built in 1744 on the Martha Brae River has some of the finest stone buildings including the remains of an imposing slave hospital: now being restored by a consortium of private investors.
PHOTO: Marcus Binney

Colbeck Castle near Old Harbour, St Catherine from the air in 1990. Built as a fortified house by Col John Colbeck in the late 1600s, it was for many years the largest building in the Caribbean.
PHOTO: Jack Tyndale Biscoe

Roaring River Great House, St Ann; fine old Edwardian building near Ocho Rios and Dunn's River Falls. This could be a very successful tourist stop for cruise ship passengers as well as for long term visitors and has been recommended for urgent restoration.
PHOTO: Marcus Binney

Another engaging aspect of Jamaica's heritage is the little houses, often delightful gingerbread confections, which are maintained with great pride and gaily painted by their occupants. Similar houses are very well illustrated in the recently published attractive book *Caribbean Style* . Clearly such houses are likely to change very quickly, and indeed, may become extinct. The best idea would be to designate one or two experimental *Gingerbread House* routes which would take people through clusters of such charming houses in pretty countryside. Going south from Montego Bay to Montpelier in St. James and then on to Woodstock in Westmoreland, a remarkable number of such houses are seen in the hill-country. The same is true of areas such as Walkerswood and Claremont in St. Ann and Black River in St. Elizabeth.

Hyde Hall, Trelawny. Away from the main north coast road, the Jamaica Heritage Trail would offer magnificent views across sugar plantations still flourishing.
PHOTO: Marcus Binney

Two storey house near New Green District in Manchester, appearing to have an inadvertent Dutch influence.
PHOTO: Wendy van Barneveld

Probably over a hundred years old, this beautiful Black River house is in danger of collapsing.
PHOTO: Pat Green (1990)

Despite out-of-context 'improvements' this split -level, hillside house near Sturge Town, St Ann is still a delight.
PHOTO: Pat Green (1990)

The painted corrugated zinc roof is perfectly acceptable on this delightful home near Pedro in St. Elizabeth.
PHOTO: Wendy van Barneveld

A delightful house near Galina Point, St Mary. Note distinctive bargeboards and interesting roof lines.
PHOTO: Pat Green (1990)

Inappropriate modifications fail to spoil this fine Black River house in the Parish of St Elizabeth.
PHOTO: Pat Green (1990)

Concrete additions have sadly altered the character of this pretty house at Tom's River in St Andrew.
PHOTO: Pat Green (1990)

A charming house with a very colourful and well planted garden at Woodstock near Darliston in Westmoreland Parish.
PHOTO: Marcus Binney

THE MAROON TRAIL

We suggest that the idea of a *Maroon Trail* and an *Emancipation Trail* be explored and developed as part of the *Heritage Trail*.

It was the Spanish who first brought slaves to Jamaica from Africa in 1513. The slaves who escaped into the forest – along with the later fugitive slaves of the British – became the indomitable Maroons who found sanctuary in the Cockpit Country and the Blue Mountains. After two wars with the British in the 1730s and 1790s, in a fierce pursuit for freedom, these proud people negotiated treaties and land grants and to this day enjoy a certain autonomy within the jurisdiction of Jamaica. Recent archaeological research is turning up new aspects of the Maroon culture including evidence that escaped Arawaks were also among the first Maroons. Their main historic towns are: Trelawny Town (now Maroon Town) in St James, Accompong in St Elizabeth, Scott's Hall in St Mary, Charles Town, Crawford Town and Moore Town in Portland.

The Maroon tradition is the only continuous element that weaves through Jamaica's history from the post-Columbian era to the present time. It was the Maroons who started the prolonged fight for freedom which culminated with full Emancipation in 1838.

Sligoville, the first ' free village' in the West Indies. The town was founded in 1835, after the emancipation of the slaves , by Rev. James M. Phillippo who also built the Baptist Church shown on top of the hill.

EMANCIPATION, 1st AUGUST 1834.

An illustration of the famous Spanish Town Square on August 1, 1838, the day that full Emancipation was declared: from the book by the English Baptist minister Rev. James M. Phillippo who was stationed at Spanish Town and was one of the activists against slavery. Phillippo was the first to establish a 'free village' for the ex-slaves. Over 200 such villages were subsequently established, mostly by non-conformist clergymen.
PHOTOS: Above and lower left: Kent Reid courtesy Raymond Brandon

THE EMANCIPATION TRAIL

The story of slavery in Jamaica is one of the most important factors in the country's history. There are two dates which are associated with the abolition of slavery in the British colonies: August 1, 1834 and August 1, 1838. The first proclamation announced immediate freedom for children, six years and under, and for domestic slaves. However, for the great majority – that is the labour force in the fields – an attempt was made to prolong forced labour by instituting a period of 'Apprenticeship' for six years. In most parts of Jamaica this was a most unsatisfactory arrangement for the 'Apprentices' and this unhappy period was brought to an end two years earlier than was originally intended, in 1838 and not 1840.

It is of interest to note that while slavery ended in Jamaica in 1838, it was not abolished in the United States of America until 1868, at the end of the Civil War.

Townships in the Jamaican hills that were established after the abolition of slavery in Jamaica could be visited on the *Emancipation Trail*. These would include Sligoville, Sturge Town, Brown's Town, and Clark's Town. Sligoville was the first free village in the West Indies. Situated in the hills of St Catherine overlooking Spanish Town, Sligoville was named after the Marquis of Sligo who, when Governor of Jamaica from 1834 to 1836, was considered sympathetic to the cause of the slaves and who had a house there.

80

An aerial view of Falmouth in 1991 looking North. This town is where William Knibb, famous Baptist missionary and abolitionist built his first chapel c.1825. Note present-day Baptist church (centre left) built in 1948 to replace the original two churches; the first destroyed during the 1831 slave rebellion, the second destroyed by hurricane in 1944. William Knibb is buried here and the church and church-yard are monuments to his memory.
PHOTO: Jack Tyndale Biscoe

The Baptist church and original theological college on the hill above Rio Bueno established by William Knibb who also founded a free village here in 1840. He died in Rio Bueno in 1845.
PHOTO: Milton Williams

A quaint confection of a church at Ramble near Porus in Manchester.
PHOTO: Wedny van Barneveld

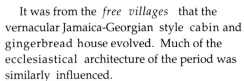

It was from the *free villages* that the vernacular Jamaica-Georgian style cabin and gingerbread house evolved. Much of the ecclesiastical architecture of the period was similarly influenced.

One of the special pleasures of Jamaica is the near certainty that one will discover something delightful whenever one ventures into the country off the beaten track. For example, we drove a few miles inland to discover at Retreat, St. Mary, a picturesque church in a very pretty churchyard overlooking the river. Next door was a handsome vernacular style building very much in need of repair (the old police station we were told) and a fine iron suspension bridge across the river. Of the Georgian church, only the tower with pretty Gothic sash-windows remain, but the whole little enclave was worth the detour. Jamaica's churches have, like many in the Caribbean, been devastated by hurricanes and though there may not be much eighteenth century work remaining, many of the churches deserve highlighting and are worth a visit. Attention should be paid, not only to the Anglican churches, but also to the Moravian, Methodist, Baptist and other non-conformist churches which played such a key role in Emancipation.

The Anglican Church and old barracks buildings at Stewart Town, Trelawny on the border of St Ann c. 1890. The town was founded in 1815 by Hon. James Stewart, Custos of Trelawny, in order to stop secret activities being carried out by slaves and freed persons in this unpopulated area between the two parishes .
PHOTO: Jamaica Archives courtesy Allan Keeling

St George's Anglican Church built between 1826 and 1860 at Mile Gully in Manchester, recently abandoned and vandalised. It was once a fashionable area near Green Vale Railway Station. Plans are being made to preserve this fine building.
PHOTOS: Wendy van Barneveld

St. Mark's Anglican Church at Rio Bueno, Trelawny consecrated in 1883.
PHOTO: Marcus Binney

THE ARAWAK NATURE TRAIL

There is much new interest in archaeological exploration of the myriad Arawak middens dotted all over the island. Even if not yet excavated, these sites should be noted, posted and protected for future investigation.

At the present time, plans are being developed for a system of protected natural areas such as National Parks, many of which include Arawak settlements yet to be explored. Studies have been submitted to Government by several eminent local and foreign experts and these are due to be formally approved and implemented by the end of 1991.

Because of the global importance of this environmental programme, funding has been made possible by USAID through the Jamaica Conservation and Development Trust and other agencies for this *Protected Areas Resource Conservation* project. Areas to be included are: Black River Lower Morass; Negril; Cockpit Country; Dolphin Head; Canoe Valley; Hellshire; Port Royal and Palisadoes; Portland Bight and Ridge; Hollymount; Worthy Park; Mason River; St. Thomas Great Morass; Blue Lagoon; Discovery Bay and Falmouth.

The vast Black River Lower Morass slated as a protected natural park and the sleepy town of Black River, once a thriving seaport with logwood as its main export product. Originally named Rio Caobana (Mahogany River) by the Spaniards, the river is 44 miles (73 kms) long and includes tributaries such as the Broad, YS, Smith, Grass, Horse and Savanna rivers. Here shown is the Broad River on the right joining the Lower Black River with the Santa Cruz Mountains and Lacovia in the distance.
PHOTO: Jack Tyndale Biscoe

San San Bay with Alligator Head at left, Pellew Island and the legendary 'bottomless' Blue Lagoon at right: 5 miles (8 km) east of Port Antonio. This unique area is of extraordinary beauty.
PHOTO: Jack Tyndale Biscoe

A logwood specimen tree in Manchester from which is derived the blue/black dye that once brought prosperity to Black River.
PHOTO: Ann Haynes Sutton

Mangroves in the St. Thomas Great Morass, one of the designated National Parks.
PHOTO: Ann Haynes Sutton

Paradise Beach near Savanna-la-Mar in Westmoreland, an unspoilt haven where Arawak people once flourished.
PHOTO: Ann Haynes Sutton

Corn Puss Gap the linking point between the westerly Blue Mountains and the John Crow Mountains in easterly St. Thomas, part of the first proposed National Park in Jamaica.
PHOTO: George Proctor, courtesy Natural History Society of Jamaica

As the routes across Jamaica are explored, it is our hope that Jamaicans and visitors alike will become increasingly aware of these several natural parks that are now being designated throughout the island. In addition to enjoying the natural beauty, glimpses of the country's distant past will add a new dimension for the inhabitants as well as for newcomers to Jamaica.

The very roads of Jamaica are an important part of the island's history. They create a network of routes through some of the most stunning and varied natural habitat. In most instances, the track and trail systems of the Arawaks eventually became Spanish bridle paths across savannas where ancient cotton trees stood sentinel; through dry river beds and gullies to hills thickly wooded with braziletto, fustic, mahogany, breadnut and bullet trees, crossing and recrossing streams and rivers and climbing to ridges, dense with forests of cedar, mahoe and santa maria; then dropping again to the plains and to the distant sea. The old Spanish road from Rio Bueno in Trelawny via Lacovia to Pedro in St. Elizabeth is one of these

Fairy Glade near Hardwar Gap in the Blue Mountains: a favourite hiking trail.
PHOTO: Wendy van Barneveld

Tree ferns in the silent mist of the Blue Mountains. Jamaica has almost 600 species of ferns many of which are not found anywhere else in the world.
PHOTO: Andreas Oberli

as well as another which ran from Martha Brae (near Falmouth) in Trelawny to Bluefields (Spanish Oristan) in Westmoreland.

With the arrival of the British in 1655, other routes tell the story of estate and parochial roads over which laden wains transported hogsheads of sugar and puncheons of rum to the 'barkaderes' and wharves of Jamaican ports. Bent on wealth through sugar production, English settlers in the new Plantation of Jamaica knew that parish roads were their life line. In every parish, records reflect the way-wardens' heavy responsibility to keep these routes open at all costs.

The saga of those whose labour actually built these roads is yet to be told; it is the saga of Jamaican road-builders during the period of slavery. Roads like the one through the spectacular Bog Walk River Gorge caused many a slave to lose his life, crushed by landslide or a single boulder as slave gangs from surrounding estates struggled against floods and other odds to keep the Sixteen Mile Walk and bridge open.

A pagan 'Duppy Tree' juxtaposed with a Christian church. A formidable Silk Cotton Tree (Ceiba pentandra) and the Methodist church in the remote town of Alexandria in the centre of the Parish of St. Ann.
PHOTO: Andreas Oberli

Sterna fuscata *a Sooty Tern: perhaps the most faithful visitor to Jamaica where it has been coming to nest for centuries.*
PHOTO: J.W. Dalling

Flat Bridge in the Bog Walk River Gorge as it was in 1778 many years after the gorge's discovery by a slave following the course of the Rio Cobre.
PHOTO: From engraving by George Robertson, courtesy National Library of Jamaica

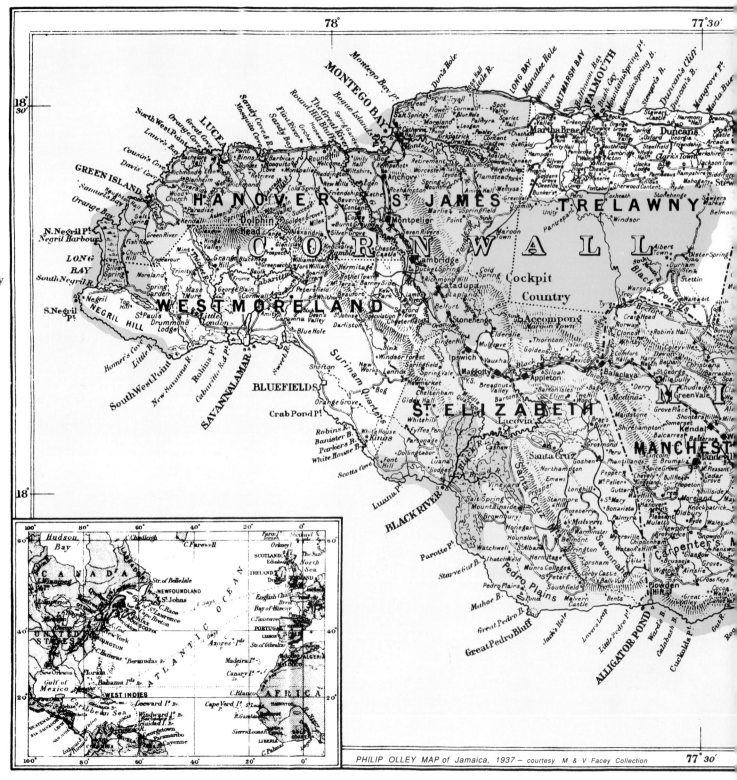

LEGEND

Proposed National Parks

Many of these areas include Arawak habitations dating from c. 600 AD

WESTMORLAND } .... { Negril Morass
HANOVER   }   { Dolphin Head

ST JAMES .... { Montego Bay
                           { Marine Park

ST ELIZABETH .... { Black River
                             { Lower Morass

ST ELIZABETH }
ST JAMES   } .... Cockpit Country
TRELAWNY   }

TRELAWNY .... Falmouth

MANCHESTER................ Canoe Valley

ST ANN .... { Discovery Bay
                               { Douglas Castle

ST CATHERINE }............... Hollymount
ST ANN   }

                           { Ocho Rios
ST. ANN .... { Marine Park
                           { Discovery Bay

CLARENDON   }   { Portland Bight
ST CATHERINE }............ { Hellshire
ST ANDREW   }   { Port Royal
                           { Palisadoes

ST MARY   }   { Blue Mountains
ST ANDREW }............... { John Crow
PORTLAND }   { Mountains
ST THOMAS }

PORTLAND .... Blue Lagoon

Map of Jamaica
from
"GUIDE TO JAMAICA"
by Philip Olley
for the Tourist Trade Development Board,
Kingston, Jamaica, B. W. I.
1937

PHILIP OLLEY MAP of Jamaica, 1937 — courtesy M & V Facey Collection

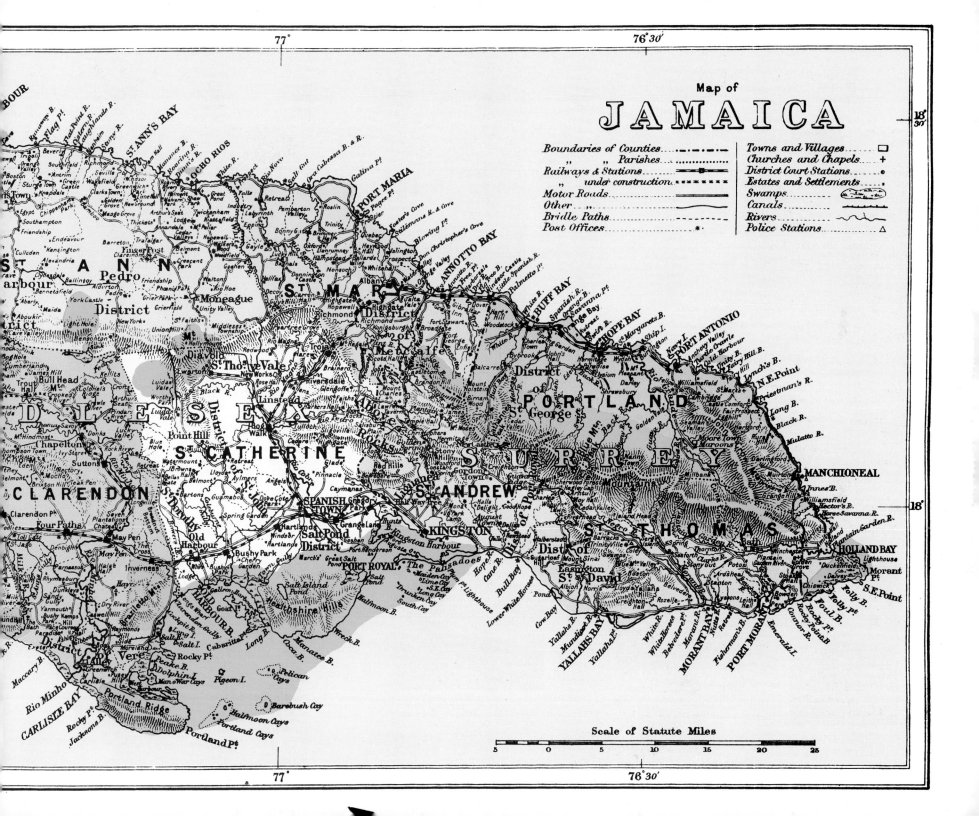

Map of
JAMAICA

Boundaries of Counties ...._._._.   Towns and Villages ......□
  „   „ Parishes ....   Churches and Chapels ...... +
Railways & Stations ......⊢S   District Court Stations ...... ⊙
  „ under construction ......   Estates and Settlements ......
Motor Roads ....   Swamps ....
Other   „   ....   Canals ....
Bridle Paths ....   Rivers ....
Post Offices ....*   Police Stations ...... △

Scale of Statute Miles
5   0   5   10   15   20   25

THE PANORAMIC TRAILWAY

The Jamaica Railway, inaugurated in 1845, has the distinction of being the first railway line outside of Europe and North America. A concerted effort should be made for the re-establishment of a modern electrical railway system to form an integral part of the *Heritage Trail*. This would alleviate many of the transportation woes of the general populace. A few airconditioned cars at an additional charge would enhance the experience of viewing the island's spectacular interior, some of which is impossible to visit by motor car.

The revamping of the railway should be a combined effort of Government and private enterprise. It should include a new route by Falmouth (which was initially bypassed and thus lost its prowess as a trading port) then go east to join the original line at Annotto Bay, possibly via Clark's Town and Brown's Town. When the railway was originally planned there was a section laid out in Trelawny between Clarke's Town and Albert Town through Barbecue Bottom and Burnt Hill in the Cockpit Country. The train tracks were never put in but it would be a simple matter to exchange the remnants of the resulting narrow road for a new railway line. Another 20-odd miles of track would take one through Wait-A-Bit and Christiana and back to the original train line at Kendall between Mandeville and Porus.

Above: Ballooning at Montpelier over the train line 10 miles (16.6 kms) from Montego Bay and 3 miles (5 kms) from the Rocklands Bird Feeding Station at Anchovy near Reading.
PHOTO: Jack Tyndale Biscoe

Middle left: Montpelier Estate in 1820 by James Hakewill. This estate, on the site of the Anglican church, was burnt during the 1831-2 slave rebellion and rebuilt in a new location situated near the present Montpelier train station.
Hakewill lithograph courtesy M. & V. Facey Collection

Below: The Appleton Estate today on the train line between Maggotty and Balaclava by the upper Black River. It is here that visitors enjoy the Appleton Rum Train Tour excursion.
PHOTO: Jack Tyndale Biscoe

Railway Station details at Kingston Terminus built in 1845 and still in use today.
PHOTO: Nadine Isaacs

Jamaica Railway in 1976: west of Balaclava in deep rural St. Elizabeth.
PHOTO: George Proctor courtesy Jamaica Natural History Society

CONCLUSION

Defunct since 1979, the old railway station at Buff Bay was built c. 1896 when the line to Port Antonio was opened. This building is typical of the rural train stations which should be preserved or rebuilt.
PHOTO: Nadine Isaacs

Another train route is needed from May Pen around the western south coast. Similarly, a route is needed east from Port Antonio to the capital city of Kingston.

The faithful restoration of the individual railway stations, old and new, is essential and these would form automatic 'check points' for the *Heritage Trail*. Each station should also include attractive snack bars and informative literature while the principal points in Kingston, Montego Bay and Port Antonio should incorporate information about the *Trail* as well as mini-museums displaying old steam engines, cabooses, turntables and other associated railway memorabilia.

Most adults and children alike are usually nostalgic about trains and a well-designed, properly-run train system could not fail to captivate locals and visitors alike while becoming a practical and viable, as well as enjoyable, form of transportation throughout the island. The very successful Appleton Rum train tour from Montego Bay to Appleton between Maggotty and Balaclava in St. Elizabeth is a case in point. Also, an additional benefit would be the reduction of traffic and wear and tear on the roads from heavy trucks once freight could be sent by rail.

As will be seen, we have proposed seven complementary components for the *Heritage Trail* which are interdependent but each maintain their own distinctive individuality:

1) *The principal historic areas of Port Royal, Spanish Town, New Seville and Falmouth*
2) *The Plantation Trail*
3) *The Gingerbread House Trail*
4) *The Maroon Trail*
5) *The Emancipation Trail*
6) *The Arawak Nature Trail*
7) *The Panoramic Trailway*

Each of these factors would have its own symbol so that signage would reflect the various individual or combination of tours to be made. Together, these elements will work as one entity. They will have the ability to grow and be improved over time while being sustained, to a considerable degree, by their own self-perpetuating income. Roads have to be maintained in the normal course of affairs, so little additional public funding will be required. If rural areas are visited more frequently and with greater appreciation, there will be more potential income to be earned by the people who inhabit these now less frequented areas.

The DeMontevin Lodge in Port Antonio. An example of a charming, modest guest house. More visitor accommodation like this would be popular while heritage buildings would be preserved at the same time.
PHOTO: Wendy van Barneveld

TOURISM ACTION PLAN's main objective is firstly to improve Jamaica's vital infrastructure to the advantage of all Jamaicans and secondly, to create a valid tourism product in today's competitive arena. In seeking to achieve these objectives, TAP expects to ensure the integrity of the country's valuable historic heritage as well as the balance of the natural ecology.

TAP's aim is to encourage sensitive overall development in the island while educating Jamaicans, who must be the guardians of their heritage, to have pride in Jamaica along with an appreciation of the country's inherent assets which if used with care can be of benefit to all.

The *Heritage Trail* will go far to achieve this goal and has the potential to bring veritable meaning to the words of Christopher Columbus when he first saw Jamaica from his caravels:

"...the fairest island that eyes have beheld..."

Railway station details c. 1896 at Port Antonio in Portland (above) and Catadupa in St. James (right).
PHOTOS: Nadine Isaacs

87

INDEX

Jamaica's Heritage - an untapped resource—Index

Jamaica's Heritage - an untapped resource—Index

Jamaica's Heritage - an untapped resource—Index

Jamaica's Heritage - an untapped resource—Index

REFERENCES
AND
ACKNOWLEDGEMENTS

CONTRIBUTORS

PATRICIA E. GREEN, Architect/Historic Preservationist, Kingston, Jamaica
ANN M. HAYNES-SUTTON, Ecologist, Mandeville, Jamaica
GEORGE R. PROCTOR, Botanist and Natural Resources Specialist, Kingston, Jamaica
RHEMA KERR, Curator, Hope Zoo, Royal Botanic Gardens, Jamaica
ANN HODGES, Architect, Kingston, Jamaica
JACKIE RANSTON, Research Consultant, Cooper's Hill, Jamaica
WENDY VAN BARNEVELD, Environmental Education Consultant, Runaway Bay, Jamaica
DAVID HARRISON, Director of Studies, Caribbean School of Architecture, Papine, Jamaica
ANTHONY AARONS, Archaeologist, Kingston, Jamaica
ANDREAS OBERLI, Director, National Arboretum Foundation, Kingston, Jamaica
KOFI AGORSAH, Edward Moulton-Barrett Lecturer in Archaeology,
        University of the West Indies, Mona, Jamaica

*In addition to the authors and the contributors the publisher
wishes to thank the following persons for their assistance:*

Douglas Armstrong	Donald Hamilton	James Parrent
Marjorie Biscoe	Barry Higman	Nora Perez
Douglas Blain	Kenneth Ingram	Geoffrey de Sola Pinto
Raymond Brandon	Nadine Isaacs	Glory Robertson
Patrick Bryan	Wendy Kuhl	Steve Solomon
David Buisseret	Edward Moulton-Barrett	Rt. Rev. Herman Spence
Audrey Downer	Christine Nunes	Robert Sutton
Roderick Ebanks	Fr Francis Osbourne, SJ	Robert K. Vincent, Jr

REFERENCES

National Library of Jamaica
Jamaica Archives
University of the West Indies Library
1878 – Jamaica Directory
Jamaica Journals – Institute of Jamaica Publications
Handbooks of Jamaica

Sloane's Natural History of Jamaica	Sir Hans Sloane	1707
Long's History of Jamaica	Edward Long	1774
The History, Civil and Commercial, of the British Colonies in the West Indies	Bryan Edwards	1793
Stark's History and Guide to Jamaica	James H. Stark	1902
Guide to Jamaica	Philip P. Olley	1937
Revels in Jamaica 1682-1838	Richardson Wright	1937
History of Jamaica	Clinton Black	1958
Exploring Jamaica - A Guide for Motorists	P. Wright & P. F. White	1969
Short History of Kingston (1692-1871)	H. P. Jacobs	1976
Short History of Clarendon	S. A. G. Taylor	1976
A - Z of Jamaican Heritage	Olive Senior	1983
Samuel Sharp - from Slave to National Hero	C. S. Reid	1988
Insight Guide's Jamaica	5th edition	1989
Birds of Jamaica	A. Downer & R. Sutton	1990

TOURISM ACTION PLAN LIMITED gratefully acknowledges the financial contribution of the undermentioned who helped to make this publication possible:
Airports Authority of Jamaica • Appliance Traders Limited • Island Dairies Limited • Jamaica National Building Society • Jamaica Promotions Limited
Ministry of Tourism (1991) • Musson (Jamaica) Limited • National Commercial Bank • Pan Jamaican Investment Trust Limited • Port Authority of Jamaica
Security Advisory Management Services • Shaw Park Beach Hotel • The Mill Press Limited • Trelawny Beach Hotel • West Indies Pulp & Paper Limited
United States Agency for International Development

This publication is available from leading bookstores in Jamaica as well as from the following organizations:

TOURISM ACTION PLAN Limited
64-70 Knutsford Boulevard
Kingston 5
JAMAICA, West Indies
Telephone: (809) 968-3626/968-3441/968-1909
Facsimile: (809) 929-5061

SAVE BRITAIN'S HERITAGE
68 Battersea High Street,
London, SW 11 3HX
ENGLAND
Telephone: (0171) 228-3336
Facsimile: (0171) 223-2714

THE MILL PRESS Limited
Constant Spring,
Box 167, Kingston 8
JAMAICA
Telephone: (809) 925-6886
Facsimile: (809) 931-1301

Proceeds from this publication will benefit restoration projects in Jamaica